Praise for
HEARING WITH THE HEART
A GENTLE GUIDE FOR DISCERNING GOD'S WILL FOR YOUR LIFE

"'Gentle' is the operative word in this title. In her hospitable and deceptively simple book, Debra Farrington serves as wise guide on the path toward discernment of God's will for us. Her highly practical suggestions and exercises are in themselves an accessible and valuable resource for anyone who has heard God's call to go deeper."

—Margaret B. Guenther, author, *Holy Listening: The Art of Spiritual Direction*

"This book on discernment of spirits will be of most help to spiritual seekers within Christian traditions who desire to be led by God as a way of life. Spiritual directors will want to recommend it to their directees as a valuable aid to grasping for themselves the central principles of discernment in highly accessible, everyday language that speaks across denominational differences. The suggested exercises for reflection are extremely helpful."

—Janet K. Ruffing, RSM, Fordham University

"Having led many retreats, Farrington knows how to communicate with those new to spiritual discernment. Profound and delightful stories—ancient, biblical, contemporary, and personal—illustrate various modes of discernment, while very do-able practices guide readers as they start down their own paths."

—Cynthia Crowner, director of the ecumenical Kirkridge Retreat Center, Bangor, Pennsylvania

"Whether we are searching for signs of God's activity in our daily lives or looking for divine guidance on the eve of making important decisions, a knowledgeable spiritual guide is an indispensable resource. By teaching us accessible, time-honored tools of discernment, Farrington trains our hearts to 'hear' and our eyes to 'see' the tug of God's often gentle yet customarily persistent presence in our lives."

—Joseph D. Driskill, associate professor of spirituality, Pacific School of Religion

"This book eases us into discernment so skillfully—with stories, prayers, and simple practices—that by the end we are eager to listen for all the ways God speaks in our lives."

—Kathleen Fischer, author and spiritual director

OTHER BOOKS BY DEBRA K. FARRINGTON

*Living Faith Day by Day: How the Sacred Rules of Monastic Traditions
Can Help You Live Spiritually in the Modern World*

One like Jesus: Conversations on the Single Life

Romancing the Holy: Gateways to Christian Experience

Unceasing Prayer: A Beginner's Guide

———

*Learning to Hear with the Heart:
Meditations for Discerning God's Will*
(JOSSEY-BASS, 2003)

HEARING

WITH THE

HEART

HEARING
WITH THE
HEART

A Gentle Guide for Discerning
God's Will for Your Life

DEBRA K. FARRINGTON

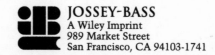

JOSSEY-BASS
A Wiley Imprint
989 Market Street
San Francisco, CA 94103-1741

Published by Jossey-Bass
A Wiley Imprint
989 Market Street, San Francisco, CA 94103-1741   www.josseybass.com

Jossey-Bass books and products are available through most bookstores. To contact Jossey-Bass directly
call our Customer Care Department within the U.S. at 800-956-7739, outside the U.S. at 317-572-3986
or fax 317-572-4002.

Jossey-Bass also publishes its books in a variety of electronic formats. Some content that appears in print may not be
available in electronic books.

Credits are on p. 247.

Library of Congress Cataloging-in-Publication Data
Farrington, Debra K.
  Hearing with the heart : a gentle guide for discerning God's will for
your life / Debra K. Farrington.—1st ed.
        p.   cm.
Includes bibliographical references and index.
  ISBN 0-7879-5959-6 (alk. paper)
  1. Christian life. 2. Discernment (Christian theology) 3.
God—Will. I. Title.
  BV4509.5 F37 2002
  248.4—dc21   2002008112

Printed in the United States of America
FIRST EDITION
HB Printing   10 9 8 7 6 5

CONTENTS

This book is for all of those who have
helped me discern and try to live
the desires of God

❀ ❀ ❀

"Knowing the reader understands that everything I say is as far from the
reality as is a painting from the living object represented, I will venture
to declare what I know."

ST. JOHN OF THE CROSS, *THE LIVING FLAME OF LOVE*

"Now if I have found favor in your sight, show me your ways,
so that I may know you and find favor in your sight."

MOSES TO GOD IN EXODUS 33:11

ACKNOWLEDGMENTS

There are always many people to thank when writing a book. Though I believe God provides the inspiration and the nudge in the first place and even provides help along the way, my community of friends and colleagues are indispensable in locating resources, thinking through the material, and getting the writing done in such a way that it makes sense to others.

For conversations, lectures, and resources that proved invaluable, I need to thank Bill Countryman, Marcus Borg, Joe Driskill, Mark Chimsky, Phyllis Tickle, Henry Carrigan, and Rebecca Langer. I thank Sheryl Fullerton, my editor at Jossey-Bass who asked me to write this, and Mark Kerr, Jessica Egbert, and Sandy Siegle, also at Jossey-Bass, for their faith in me and for the invitation to write this book. Sheryl was as insightful as she was kind while this book was being written, and I am deeply grateful for her help and support. And an author couldn't ask for better cheerleaders and supportive marketing help than I've received from Mark, Jessica, and Sandy. My thanks go to the "behind the scenes" people, too, for their expert and elegant work: Joanne Clapp Fullagar and her team of experts, and Lisa Buckley, who designed this lovely book. As always, I thank my agent, Linda Roghaar, who takes care of business so I don't have to and who never seems to tire of supporting my work.

Harrisburg, Pennsylvania
October 2002

DEBRA K. FARRINGTON

INTRODUCTION

"I'm not sure whose idea it was to write this book," I complained to a friend one day while wrestling with a chapter that wasn't coming together. I never set out to write a book on discernment, not consciously anyway. My editor at Jossey-Bass approached me and asked me to work on this topic. "It is underneath all the other work you've done," she said. And she was right, but I'm not sure the idea was originally hers either. God is tricky, I've found, though not in a mean-spirited, hurtful way. But God has been wonderfully effective at pointing me in directions that have come as complete surprises. And God isn't above using editors to get the work done either.

Writing a book on discernment has been so much harder than any other topic I've tried to explore in print. I began to write about discernment as something one does at those major crossroads of life but realized that you can't listen well at those times if you've never thought about discernment as part of your life as a whole. So I added a whole new section to the book—a section about discernment as a way of living. But throughout all of the writing, just when I thought I had something useful to say, a bit of fine print jumped out at me, and I wanted to qualify everything to within an inch of its life. Even though it appears that hard-and-fast rules about discerning God's will for your life don't exist, we have to do our best to try to understand, just as the disciples did in this story:

The disciples were full of questions about God.

Said the master: "God is the Unknown and the Unknowable. Every statement made about him, every answer to your questions, is a distortion of the truth."

The disciples were bewildered. "Then why do you speak about him at all?"

"Why does the bird sing?" said the master.[1]

In this book, we'll be like the master here and explore discernment because we have to. To avoid asking how we discern God's will is like asking the bird not to sing. The epigraph from Saint John of the Cross, which appears at the beginning of this book, says it all: I trust you know that what I have to say is just a loose approximation of the reality of discernment. Only practice and time spent in discerning God's will for your own life can truly teach you the way. Still, I hope you find these pointers and suggestions helpful.

Though all journeys through discernment will be different in the particulars, there is one instruction they share: it is difficult and dangerous to journey alone. Even the most spiritually mature person needs the companionship of other people as he or she learns to open the heart to God. We have a tendency to want to "do it ourselves" in this culture; sometimes that is wise, even exciting. But discerning God's desires for our lives is a journey full of twists and turns and sometimes confusion. I strongly encourage you to find a spiritual community or director, or some other wise companion who has taken this journey before, as you choose to practice discernment in your life.

Very early in my life I learned another simple but important lesson that informs this book: no one has all the answers. There's no such thing as one system or one way of understanding that works for everyone. I learned that lesson as a result of my mother's need to explore a variety of faiths when I was a child and my own searches as an adult. By the time I was fourteen, I had been Unitarian, Presbyterian, and Jewish. As an adult, I explored the Presbyterian Church again and the United Church of Christ. I finally landed in the Episcopal Church a decade or so ago, where I am at home. Later in my life, I worked for a consortium of nine seminaries, ranging from Unitarian to Catholic, along with several centers focused on Buddhism, Judaism, and other faith perspectives. What I learned along the way is that everyone has access to a part of the Truth. I continue to find that valuable in my faith life, and though I am quite at home in the Episcopal Church, I still look to Roman Catholics, Protestants of many denominations, and other traditions for enlightenment.

So perhaps it is not by chance that this exploration of the art of discerning God's will draws on a wide variety of approaches. In my own experiences and in the reading I've done, I've found parts of the various explanations of discernment to be helpful, while other parts made little sense to me. Consequently, this book includes material from a variety of perspectives. The Desert Fathers, Ignatius, the Quakers—even contemporary understandings of personality—all find a place in these pages. I'm making the assumption that you, like me, will find some of what I have to offer here helpful, while other parts may be less intriguing for you. But I hope that, no matter who you are, some parts of the various approaches found here will nurture and inform you, that they will open up and nourish your heart and your relationship with God.

HEARING
WITH THE
HEART

Part One

BEGINNING
THE
JOURNEY

Chapter One

THE HEARING HEART

Grant me, O Lord, to know what I ought to know, to love what I ought to love, to praise what delights you most, to value what is precious in your sight, to hate what is offensive to you. Do not allow me to judge according to the sight of my eyes, nor to pass sentence according to the hearing of my ears; but to discern with a true judgment between things visible and spiritual, and above all things, always to inquire what is the good pleasure of your will.[1]

THOMAS À KEMPIS

When Solomon was still a new king, God came to him in a dream one night and told him to ask for whatever he needed from God (1 Kings 3). Solomon could have asked for anything—wealth, long life, or anything else—but he asked for only one thing: a "hearing heart" with which to discern good from evil. With a hearing heart, Solomon could judge rightly. Various versions of the Bible translate Solomon's request as one for wisdom or for an understanding mind or heart, but the literal Hebrew translation of Solomon's request is "hearing heart." Solomon wants—and is given—a heart that does more than listen; it hears with compassion, and it knows God's will.

The ancient Hebrews thought of the heart differently than we do today. The heart was not just a physical organ to them; it was the center of the whole human being, including everything physical, intellectual, and psychological. Emotions, feelings, moods, passions, thought, understanding, and wisdom were all thought to reside in the heart. Most important, it was within the heart that people truly met God's word—where real knowledge and conversion took place.[2] So when Solomon asked God for a hearing heart, he was really asking for God's word to reside in his heart—for God's word to inform everything Solomon felt, knew, and thought. Because he had a hearing heart, Solomon became a wise and discerning king. But the gift of a hearing heart was not reserved for Solomon alone; we, too, can have a hearing heart—one that knows God and discerns well.

You shall love the Lord your God with all your heart, and with all your soul, and with all your mind.

MATTHEW 22:37

To discern means more than to understand or to make a decision. *Discern* comes from the Latin *discernere*; *dis* means apart, and *cernere* means to separate. Thus, from all of the options before us, we "separate apart" those that seem uniquely suited to us. We do that when making a decision as well, but discernment, at least in Christian spirituality, implies that we take God's will for us into account rather than simply our own desires.

Hearing with the Heart

It isn't that we ignore our deepest desires. In fact, we have to learn to listen to them with great attentiveness and respect, because God often speaks through the desires of our hearts. "What therefore thou findest that thy soul desireth in following God, that do, and keep thy heart," writes one of the Desert Fathers.[3] If we cannot listen to our heart, discernment of God's will is difficult if not impossible. But once we have learned to listen to and hear our heart's desires, then we ask the question: Are these desires speaking of God's will for me and for the world around me?

That may sound like a simple question. If you are a religious person, you have probably heard people describe an event as being "God's will" without thinking about it or doubting for a second that it was. But discernment is a subtle and intentional art that requires openness to the Spirit and a little bit of practice. It is as easy and as difficult as learning to hear, see, feel, and think with your heart.

A PERVASIVELY PRESENT GOD

To begin talking about discerning God's will requires that we be clear about what we believe about God and God's will for us. For some of us, the phrase "God's will" evokes images or impressions of a puppeteer God who lives somewhere on high, holding and manipulating the strings that cause us to have car accidents, to find the perfect parking place, or to heal or die from an illness. This God has lots of rules and is one who, like Santa Claus, rewards us for being good and punishes us for being bad. At times this is a wrathful God—the one whom we blame for the earthquakes, fires, floods, and other "acts of God," as the insurance companies call them. We've all heard people who speak about God in this way, as when a young couple who has just lost a newborn child is told that God must have wanted their baby, or when we imply that God has a secret purpose, unfathomable to us, for everything that happens to us, good or bad. This kind of God appears to have only one particular plan for each of us, and so our task is to guess—more than discern—exactly what God wants us to do, how we should do it, and when we should be finished. The consequences for guessing incorrectly are usually dire.

The puppeteer God, however, is not the one I know, love, and trust. When I speak of God's will in this book, I do not mean a deity who has a single set of plans for each individual in this world. This is not a God who decides that I will have a car accident this evening or who has only one job in mind for me. Rather, I believe in a God who loves me and has given me free will to make choices. God is not someone or something "out there" but is the one in whom I "live and move and have my being" (Acts 17:28). God dwells in everything around me, as well as within me. God loves me. I am the daughter with whom God is well pleased, and the same is true for you. God cares passionately about my welfare and about yours as well.

When we try to describe our relationship with God, one of the most difficult aspects is that we have no way to describe God's actions if God is not a being like us. We say, for instance, that we hear God's voice, but that is a pale reflection of how we experience God "speaking" to us. We talk about feeling guided by God's will, but we don't usually mean that God handed us a piece of paper or sent us an e-mail telling us exactly what to do. We end up speaking about God as if we were talking about a person or being like us, but we do so with the understanding that we are speaking in metaphors, which is the best we can do.

One of the loveliest metaphors to help us visualize this in-dwelling sense of God is water. Marjorie Hewitt Suchocki, a contemporary theologian, suggests that we think of God as water and ourselves as living within the water. She so aptly describes it this way:

> Water rushes to fill all the nooks and crannies available to it; water swirls around every stone, sweeps into every crevice, touches all things in its path—and changes all things in its path. The changes are subtle, often slow, and happen through a continuous interaction with the water that affects both the water and that which the water touches. . . . The water doesn't exert its power by being "single-minded" over and above [the things within it], but simply by being pervasively present to and with all things.[4]

This image of "God as water" is the one we will keep before us in this book. God flows in and around all that exists, being pervasively present to everything. Of course, God is also intentional in a way that water is not. But still, if we think about it, water as a presence—taken for granted by the creations that live within it—speaks clearly about our own relationship to God and the discernment skills we'll explore here. One of the main tasks of discernment is to learn to be as equally present to God as God is to us.

THE DESIRE OF GOD

To be as present to God as God is to us is to pay attention to what we perceive to be God's will—God's desire—and to act on that. The New Testament speaks of this beautifully, for example, in Ephesians 1:17–18: "I pray that the God of our Lord Jesus Christ, the Father of glory, may give you a spirit of wisdom and revelation as you come to know him, so that, *with the eyes of your heart enlightened, you may know what is the hope to which he has called you*" (italics mine).

Take delight in the LORD, and he will give you the desires of your heart.

PSALM 37:4

You are indeed my rock and my fortress; for your name's sake lead me and guide me.

PSALM 31:3

Ephesians' "hope" is what I think of as God's desire for all of us. And that hope, the passage says, echoing earlier biblical texts, can only be understood with the eyes of our enlightened hearts. God calls us, which means that God invites us—even entices us—into something extraordinary. As we come to know and love God, we find ourselves caring about what God desires, just as we care about the hopes and desires of people we love. Our task is to use the gifts of the heart to discover—to discern—what God asks each of us to be or do as individuals and then to choose to act in ways that bring that vision to life instead of working against it. When we begin to "separate apart" the call—the hope of God—that is uniquely ours, we are suddenly like fish swimming with the current instead of against it. We discover energy and creativity we never knew we had—energy and creativity we may have wasted in trying to swim upstream.

Bill Countryman speaks powerfully about this misuse of energy in his book, *Gifted by Otherness: Gay and Lesbian Christians in the Church.* For many years he was not aware of being gay, and even upon recognizing that fact, it took him quite a while to process it, especially because he was active in the church as a priest. But as he came to know who he was and to what God had called him, life became much clearer:

> As soon as I acknowledged this sexuality, life became clearer and simpler and richer. . . . I had all kinds of energy—spiritually, intellectually, and emotionally—that I hadn't experienced before because it was tied up in concealing myself from myself. My sense of communion with God deepened. And all of this was rooted in the experience of consenting to a truth I had been avoiding.[5]

Bill had finally listened to his heart—to his own desire and to God's desire—so he no longer needed to spend his energy pushing God away.

Trying to live without discerning and acting on God's will is very difficult, as Bill's story illustrates. Think of it as driving with your car's wheels out of alignment. You have to hang on to the steering wheel with all your might to keep the car going straight instead of wobbling around the road. But when the wheels—when we ourselves—are properly aligned, driving the car is easier, not to mention safer.

Fifth-century Desert Father John Cassian sums up the dangers for any monk who fails to try to understand and act on God's will:

So you see, then, that the gift of discernment is neither earthly nor of little account, but is, rather, a very great boon of divine grace. And if a monk does not do his utmost to acquire it and he does not have a clear knowledge of the spirits rising up against him he will surely stray like someone in a dark night amid gruesome shadows and not only will he stumble into dangerous pits and down steep slopes but he will often fall even in the level, straightforward places.[6]

Although Cassian was writing about monks, the passage applies to us as well.

❊ ❊ ❊

Practicing the art of discerning God's will and living by it does not prevent us from straying into dangerous pits and down steep slopes. But our new eyes and ears may help us avoid many of the hazards, and they will certainly help us walk with clearer vision in the level places. Living in alignment with God's will rather than resisting it frees up what is best in us.

Two examples of nonalignment with God's will are trying to do a job that does not use your skills or gifts or trying to stay in a relationship that does not work well. You become drained. If you've ever worked in a job that was simply wrong for you or if you've been in a relationship that was not nurturing, you have a sense of what I mean. You could expend everything you have trying to fit the proverbial square peg into the round hole. The same is true of the effort to live a life that is not in accordance with God's desires. Discerning and acting on God's will does not mean you'll never have difficult days or feel lousy sometimes. But choosing to live in alignment with God makes you more joyful, compassionate, and peaceful, even on the bad days.

Discerning God's will, of course, isn't as easy as flipping a light on. God's desires sometimes seem like a gigantic jigsaw puzzle—one with a trillion pieces—with no picture of the complete puzzle on the outside of the box. How would you start piecing God's desires for you together? With a jigsaw puzzle, you would look for the pieces with a straight edge and try to put the borders of the picture in place. Then you would study the pieces carefully, looking for pieces that seem to fit together. Using a combination of reason, logic, and intuition, and, if you're smart, a lot of help from others, you would begin to put the picture together little by little.

> *You desire truth in the inward being; therefore teach me wisdom in my secret heart.*
>
> PSALM 51:6

We do something similar to that in learning to hear with the heart. We begin to piece together a picture of God's will through spiritual practices. We learn prayer practices and attentiveness to our bodies, dreams, and gifts, all of which help us listen for, understand, and open up to God's call. We ask what others have learned about the will of God, sometimes by studying what others have written and sometimes by listening to the wise ones among us. Reason and logic have a place in our discernment, as do feelings and intuition. All of these help us find the correct "puzzle pieces" and put them in the right location; bits and pieces of the picture begin to come together. Along the way, we'll probably force two puzzle pieces together that don't actually fit together and lose track of the overall picture. Sometimes we have to backtrack and start over. But gradually, a sense of the whole picture and where we fit in it emerges. We come to know, as Paul wrote, the hope to which God has called us.

And though we might tend to think of the great biblical characters as having some kind of special channel to God, each and every one of us has access to what God desires. Perhaps it is like a forgotten memory—something we can catch glimpses of at the edges of our consciousness, just as we remember bits and pieces of our dreams at the moment of waking.

Maybe you've heard a story that has been circulating for a number of years. Two parents come home from the hospital and introduce their five-year-old daughter to her new baby brother. The girl insists on being left alone with the baby, which causes the parents a good bit of anxiety. The young child persists in her demands, however, and the parents finally concede, leaving the intercom on in the baby's room so they can intervene if necessary. The five-year-old, finally alone with her baby brother, speaks to him with these words: "Tell me what the voice of God sounds like. I've almost forgotten."

I have no idea if this story is factual, but I find great truth in it. Deep in our souls somewhere we all know the voice of God and God's will for us, but we allow ourselves to be convinced that we do not. An abusive parent convinces a child that she is unworthy of God's attention. An authority figure tells us what we should believe about God and chases away our inner knowing the same way we type over words on the computer screen, erasing what was there originally. Or we get so enslaved to the tasks and responsibilities of daily life that we forget to make time to even think about the will of God.

Even so, God's voice lives within each one of us. It is more than just a vague memory; it is a promise, a calling out to us, from the "Dreamer"—God—who loves us more deeply than we can imagine. "Are there any of us the Dreamer has dreamed into being that the Dreamer does not want to come true?" writes Robert Benson, a contemporary spiritual writer.[7] And the answer is no. God wants all of us to "come true"—to find our place in creation and live it fully. That is what discernment is about. It is separating God's hope, desire, and will from the clamor of the rest of life and focusing on that.

NEW EYES, NEW EARS, NEW HEARTS

In his classic children's story *The Little Prince,*[8] Antoine de Saint-Exupéry shows us what it is like to use the eyes and ears of the heart. The little prince wanders from planet to planet, meeting characters—caricatures of all of us—who think they know what is important. But the prince never stops on any one planet for very long. Then on one planet, the little prince befriends a rose and meets her every need until he is worn out with her demands and leaves her. On another planet, he meets a fox that insists that the little prince tame him, which the prince does. But then, when it is time to go, the fox is sad because the fox and the little prince care for one another now. The fox has taught the little prince that compassion and caring are more important than any of the other things the prince has encountered. Although the people the prince has met on the various planets call themselves successful because they can quantify what they've accomplished, the fox knows that these successes mean relatively little, that it is the relationship between the prince and the fox that is truly important. "It is only with the heart that one can see rightly," the fox tells the little prince. "What is essential is invisible to the eye."

Discernment is about seeing—as in understanding—the essential things that are invisible to our normal eyes and ears. We cannot discern God's desires for us and for the world unless we use the eyes and ears of our hearts, any more than the little prince could see what was important just by observing how the various people lived on the planets he visited.

In the New Testament, Jesus speaks constantly about seeing in a whole new way if we want to hear the voice of God whispering (or hollering) to us. In Matthew 13, he tells the disciples that he speaks to them in parables because "seeing they do not perceive, and hearing they do not listen, nor do they understand."

> With them indeed is fulfilled the prophecy of Isaiah that says: "You will indeed listen, but never understand, and you will indeed look, but never perceive. For this people's heart has grown dull, and their ears are hard of hearing, and they have shut their eyes, so that they might not look with their eyes, and listen with their ears, and understand with their heart and turn—and I would heal them." (Matthew 13:13-15)

These people's hearts have grown so dull that their eyes don't actually perceive anything, and their ears hear very little. If they would only open their eyes—actually, if they would only open their hearts—Jesus would heal them.

Throughout the gospels, Jesus continues to drive his point home. In Matthew 20:30–34, Jesus gives sight to those who ask:

There were two blind men sitting by the roadside. When they heard that Jesus was passing by, they shouted, "Lord, have mercy on us, Son of David!" The crowd sternly ordered them to be quiet; but they shouted even more loudly, "Have mercy on us, Lord, Son of David!" Jesus stood still and called them, saying, "What do you want me to do for you?" They said to him, "Lord, let our eyes be opened." Moved with compassion, Jesus touched their eyes. Immediately they regained their sight and followed him.

Throughout the gospels of Matthew, Mark, and Luke, Jesus repeatedly reminds us, "Let those with ears, listen!" At moments when Jesus is most exasperated, or perhaps saddened, with the disciples' inability to understand, he speaks of the hardened heart: "Do you still not perceive or understand? Are your hearts

O God, grant us in all our doubts and uncertainties the grace to ask what you would have us do; that the spirit of wisdom may save us from all false choices, and that in your light we may see light, and in your straight path may not stumble, through Jesus Christ our Lord.

WILLIAM BRIGHT

hardened? Do you have eyes, and fail to see? Do you have ears, and fail to hear?" (Mark 8:17–18). The hardened heart is the problem. It cannot see or hear.

We tend to read these stories and references as ones about people who actually cannot see or hear—and they are. But they are also about those who cannot understand what Jesus is doing or hear what he is actually saying. They are stories about those who fail to understand what Jesus is trying to teach them about the will of a compassionate God rather than a legalistic one. Jesus is trying to tell these folks the Good News—that God loves them, all of them—but some of the crowd can only concentrate on God's laws. These stories from the New Testament point us toward the kinds of sensibilities and abilities we will need if we are to understand the art of discernment. We must nurture the "eyes of the heart" that Paul speaks of in Ephesians. We must learn to see and hear the world through the eyes, ears, and heart of God.

DESIRING THE GIFT

Open my eyes that I may see
Glimpses of truth thou hast for me;
Place in my hands the wonderful key
That shall unclasp and set me free.
Open my ears that I may hear
Voices of truth thou sendest clear,
And while the wave notes fall on my ear
Everything false will disappear.

Hearing with the Heart

Silently now I wait for thee,
Ready by God, thy will to see;
Open my eyes, illumine me,
Spirit divine.

CLARA H. SCOTT

Nurturing these abilities involves, first and foremost, *desiring* to see and hear clearly and filtering out all the obstacles that stand in the way of doing so. Clara H. Scott, the author of the hymn just quoted, knew about that desire when she wrote about eyes and ears focused on God. She knew that in order to know the hope of God, we must learn to listen to what our own heart desires instead of what the world tells us we *should* desire, for God often speaks to us through the yearning in our heart. There is a deep distrust of this in some circles today, with good reason. Rampant individualism that focuses only on what you or I want can easily become egotism and run counter to God's will for us.

> *Speak, Lord, for your*
> *servant hears.*
> *Grant us ears to hear,*
> *Eyes to see,*
> *Wills to obey,*
> *Hearts to love;*
> *Then declare what you will,*
> *Reveal what you will,*
> *Command what you will,*
> *Demand what you will.*
>
> CHRISTINA ROSSETTI

This has been true for a long time. In the fifth century, John Cassian recorded a story about a man named Hero who spent fifty years living in total seclusion in the desert, "keeping to the rigors of abstinence with a severity that was outstanding." Hero was one of many men and women who fled to the Egyptian desert in the third and fourth centuries, seeking a deeper connection with God, free from all secular or material concerns and needs.

Although they usually lived out of earshot and eyesight from one another, they were loosely organized into communities and frequently came together on Sundays or holy days to worship. But Hero (as Abba Moses told Cassian and Germanus) felt that worshiping and eating with others, even on the Sabbath or feast days, gave the impression that he was relaxing his strict disciplines, so he kept entirely to himself.

Hero believed that he could discern God's guidance unassisted, outside of any community whatsoever, and so he lived that way. One day, Hero discerned that God wanted him to jump into a very deep well as a test of faithfulness. According to Abba Moses,

> [Hero] threw himself headlong into a well. . . . He did so trusting completely in the assurance of the angel who had guaranteed that on account of the merit of his virtues and of his works he could never come to any harm. To experience his undoubted freedom from danger the deluded man threw himself in the darkness of night into this well. He would know at first hand the great merit of his own virtue when he emerged unscathed. He was pulled out half-dead by his brothers.[9]

Give us, O Lord, a steadfast heart, which no selfish desires may drag downwards; give us an unconquered heart, which no troubles can wear out; give us an upright heart, which no unworthy ambitions may tempt aside. Give us also, O Lord our God, understanding to know you, perseverance to seek you, wisdom to find you, and a faithfulness that may finally embrace you; through Jesus Christ our Lord. Amen.

THOMAS AQUINAS

Hero died two days later. As he was dying, the other monks tried to convince Hero that he had not actually heard the voice of God, but to no avail. His spiritual arrogance was so great that not even the threat of imminent death could convince Hero that he had listened to Satan instead of God.

Like so many of us, Hero proudly thought he was listening to the voice of God when it turned out that he was really hearing his own ego, or Satan, as Cassian says. Sometimes listening to our heart's desires can lead us to act wrongly, as Hero did, so we are right to be cautious about them. But assuming that our focus is on God in the first place and that we are part of a community that can offer corrections to our vision when needed—something Hero spurned—our hearts often speak to us of what God desires most. Instead of dismissing what speaks most deeply to us, we need to ask if these desires might be speaking to us of God's will. We'll explore how to do that throughout this book.

Christian, in John Bunyan's classic book *The Pilgrim's Progress,*[10] teaches us a little about paying attention to and following our heart. Weighed down by the burdens of his life and desperate to be rid of them, he sets out to find another way to live. At the beginning of the journey, Evangelist points Christian to the path to God, which Christian has trouble seeing clearly at first. But he desires to be rid of his load so deeply that he sets out toward a goal he sees only dimly, according to Evangelist's instructions. At various junctures along the way, he loses track of the real goal, the real desire; instead of following Evangelist's instructions, he tries shortcuts suggested by others. Each time he veers from the correct path, he has to struggle to catch sight of the way again. Logic and reason are of little use to him in staying focused on God; advisers along the way give him logical arguments for pursuing other paths and show Christian (who is using his ordinary eyes to see) goals other than God. Only when he uses the eyes of his heart—the ones that set him on his path originally, the ones that speak of desire and hope—does he stay on the right path and filter out all the distractions.

Christian's story points to the principle that we must be willing to ask for our new eyes and ears or at least be willing to accept them when offered. Christian is brave enough—and it does take courage—to ask Evangelist for help. Maybe we can imagine Christian being so burdened that he summons the courage to ask Evangelist for help. But consider the two blind men in the Matthew 20 story mentioned earlier who asked Jesus to open their eyes. These men had spent their lives begging for their living and probably knew no other life. Having regained their sight, after asking for it, they could no longer live in the old ways any more than Christian could. They all would have to walk new paths from that time forward. To be willing to ask for and receive the gift of new sight and new ways of hearing requires courage to change and to trust in finding one's own way on a new path. We'll look at this in the next chapter.

EVERYDAY DISCERNMENT

Often the discussion of discernment seems to imply that discernment has to do with life's big decisions, such as marriage or vocation. Yet, although seeking God's guidance for major decisions is certainly appropriate and wise, we need not save discernment for those big moments. It would probably be silly, not to mention time consuming, to try to discern whether parking your car in this place or that helps further heaven on earth, but it is important to discern what to do with the gifts—financial and otherwise—that we possess. How and when to pray; how to treat others; how to nurture friendships, our spiritual lives, our employees and colleagues; how to vote; how to help those in our communities who have few resources; how to spend the money we have—all these activities and decisions benefit from prayer and conversation with God. In this way, each of us is called to be a partner, or co-creator, with God in building up our world.

> *Take delight in the LORD, and he will give you the desires of your heart.*
>
> PSALM 37:4

Each of us, as God's co-creator, must take responsibility for listening for God's guidance. No one can do that for us. And we must take responsibility for acting on that guidance as well. Imagine what the world would become if we all— every creature—truly felt like partners with God in creating heaven on earth.

Perhaps it seems prideful to think that you have a role to play in bringing about the kind of world that God truly desires. But you bear no more and no less responsibility than every other living being in the world. God desires that we all play our part in coming into our own as a co-creator with God. And once we have experienced God as a deity who

> *The LORD is my strength and my shield; in him my heart trusts; so I am helped, and my heart exults, and with my song I give thanks to him.*
>
> PSALM 28:7

loves us unconditionally, as God our Beloved, then it is only natural to want, for the world, what God wants. Much as we want what is best for our children, our partners, and our close friends, we must also share and act on God's will for a just and beautiful creation.

I once heard that winds around the world are capable of bringing dust from Africa to Colorado. No country or people can isolate themselves as easily as they might think. Acting or not acting on God's behalf works much the same way. When we do something hateful, hurtful, and cruel to someone else, that act, or the spirit of it, spreads from the victim to someone else, and it ripples outward like the small waves made by a stone thrown in a pond. When we practice kindness, concern, and graciousness, the same is true. It spreads to others. Each act is just a small thing, but it can further God's will or help to defeat it.

As overwhelming as that sounds, if we don't help build up the earth, we are part of the world's problems of violence, hatred, cruelty, and carelessness. As Catholic priest William Barry says, when we give up trying to help and write off the possibilities of our being co-creator with God as naïve, doing so "sanctions the *status quo* of mistrust and enmity between people whom God wants to be brothers and sisters and it takes us off the hook of trying to find ways to live out God's dream."[11] Idealistic as it may seem, without our cooperation and assistance, God cannot continue to create a world of justice and love.

> *God be in my head, and in my understanding;*
> *God be in my eyes, and in my looking;*
> *God be in my mouth, and in my speaking;*
> *God be in my heart, and in my thinking;*
> *God be at my end, and at my departing.*
>
> ANONYMOUS

If we choose to be co-creators (and it is a choice; God does not coerce our co-operation), we can help bring into being a world where peace, love, and charity rule, where we actually embody God. We become God's hands and feet and voices. So when we help clean rubbish off the beach, work at the local soup kitchen, comfort someone who mourns, or delight in someone's accomplishments—and other everyday kinds of activities—we give God a body in this world. In doing these things and so many others, we take action on what God wills for us and for the world, and we remember and fulfill our role as co-creators.

That does not imply that we spend every moment of every day trying to discern whether or not or how to do the tasks in front of us. I do not look at every single piece of correspondence that I receive in a day and spend a half hour discerning how God would have me answer this or that e-mail. But to live as God would have us live, we need to learn to listen, see, and feel with our hearts—actions and qualities we'll explore in the rest of this book. Once we have begun to listen and see with our new ears and eyes, we can more easily look at the tasks or needs in front of us and choose to act in a way that is in accordance with God's deepest desires.

Learning to discern and discerning well are tasks we will never complete in this lifetime. We can't just learn and memorize a sequence of letters in an alphabet, get our A+ from the teacher, and be done. In fact, it is likely that, this side of the grave, we will never know for sure if we have truly discerned God's desires for us. As Paul writes in 1 Corinthians, "For now we see in a mirror, dimly, but then we will see face to face. Now I know only in part; then I will know fully, even as I have been fully known" (1 Corinthians 13:12). One of the surest signs of discerning poorly is being absolutely, positively certain that we know God's will. If we feel we know God's will for us in a particular situation with 90 percent certainty, with a little bit of room for doubt in our hearts and minds, that is probably the best we can hope for in this life.

More often than not, we will not be close to that 90 percent level of conviction. I hope, however, that by the end of this book you will be a little bit closer to knowing God's desires than you are today and that you will have discovered some new skills and an increased openness to help you grow in faithfulness.

GETTING STARTED

The remainder of this book is about exploring the skills and the "eyes of the heart" that you will need to learn the art of discernment. The rest of Part One explores the "big picture" issues—the things you need to know about living a life shaped by the discernment of God's will. First and foremost is learning to open your heart and trust in God's ways, which flies in the face of the self-sufficiency we are often taught to value. Chapter Two looks at the kinds of individual and cultural difficulties that prevent us from being open to listening and trusting God as a partner.

In Part Two, we'll look at some of the basic tools you'll need to practice discernment, particularly everyday discernment. Learning the skills of discernment before you are at a crossroad in your life will help you discern better when you face a big decision. In Part Two, we'll look at prayer and the art of paying attention, studying, and having spiritual companionship as they relate to discerning well. Each chapter in Part Two (as well as Part Three) includes actual practices for you to experiment with and learn. If you'd like more detail on any of them, you'll find some suggested resources at the end of the book.

In Part Three, we'll turn to some specific skills you may need at major crossroads. Chapters Seven through Nine explore particular skills that are required in discernment: reason, intuition, imagination, group support, patience, and action. The balancing of all of these skills is essential to clear discernment. Chapter Ten examines how to know, as best you can, if you have discerned well. Blessings on your journey!

Chapter Two

NAVIGATING THE
OBSTACLE COURSE

Why do you call me "Lord, Lord," and do not do what I tell you?

LUKE 6:46

Writer Anne Lamott, in *Traveling Mercies,* tells a story of how one day at the beach she saw a man repeatedly beat his golden retriever with a stick. A little whisper came out of her throat demanding that the man stop, but his viciousness terrified her, and she was frozen in place. "I knew on the beach that Jesus would have stepped in to save the dog," she writes, "and he would have been loving the dog beater as he did so. He would have been seeing the dog beater's need and fear. Well, I am certainly not there yet."[1] Many of us are "not there yet" either and, as with Lamott, it isn't for lack of trying.

Paying attention to God's desires and acting on them can be downright difficult sometimes. It would be easier to ignore God, forget about God's vision, and just go our own way sometimes. Seeing and hearing with the heart, with compassion, is sometimes painful, as Lamott's story demonstrates. But as we come to know and love God more deeply, paying attention to and acting on God's guidance becomes more of a joy than a burden. God invites us to listen with our heart all the time, even on the beach, and not just at the major crossroads of our lives. Listening for God's call, or invitation, is the practice of discernment.

But as wonderful as God's call is, it can be difficult to respond to it fully. As Lamott found out when fears for her safety and for the safety of her son interfered with her ability to stop the violence in front of her, there are all sorts of barriers, personal and societal, that get in the way of our discerning and responding to the call of God.

I AM GOD'S WHAT?

For some of us, the most difficult barrier to practicing discernment is believing that God would have anything to say to us in the first place. If I asked you to say out loud that God loves you unconditionally, just as you are, could you do it? Some of us have been so bruised by images of a power-hungry and judgmental God who waits to punish us for each and every sin we commit that we have trouble believing that God seeks us out as a partner.

A friend of mine, raised in a tradition that encourages belief in a demanding God who tolerates no deviation from the straight and narrow path, has trouble

Hearing with the Heart

leaving that behind, much as she wants to. She listens to me talk about discerning the will of God but remains skeptical that there is anything more to understand than the rules she was taught as a child. For people raised in this way, living God's way is more a question of following the rules—though the rules vary from church to church—than it is of being asked, as a beloved child of God, to help make God's desires a reality. Very little is required by way of discernment; the rules are generally handed down sternly from the pulpit and transmitted through teachers and parents. In this worldview, life is less about being God's beloved than it is about being good and obeying the rules established within the community.

Let me hear of your steadfast love in the morning, for in you I put my trust. Teach me the way I should go, for to you I lift up my soul.

PSALM 143:8

Adults who were not loved or treated well as children can also find it difficult to believe that God loves them and desires their participation in an ongoing creation. Our images of God are often influenced by our experience of our parents; if our parents do not love us or if they abuse us, we have trouble imagining that God loves us. Roberta Bondi, in her remarkable book *Memories of God,* talks about being confused, as a young child, about the difference between her earthly father and her heavenly Father.

> I loved my father so much, yet I knew I could never please him. I was angry with him and guilty over my poisonous secret, anger. I could not possibly believe my human father loved me as I was. And if this was true of my earthly father, how much more must this be the case with my

heavenly Father. Surely my heavenly Father's standards for females had to be stricter than my earthly father's.[2]

Especially as young children, we form our self-image based on what our parents and other authority figures say about us or what their actions (or lack of actions) tell us. Once we see ourselves as a bad child or as a person who is unlovable, we tend to universalize that feeling and believe that everyone, even God, sees us this way. That feeling of unworthiness makes it difficult to know a loving God who wants us as a partner.

In an article on discernment, contemporary spirituality writer Wendy Wright recounts a sermon she heard on how Jesus' knowledge of himself as God's beloved helped him discern God's voice from the voice of the Devil in the wilderness. Right before Jesus was led into the wilderness, he was baptized, and the Spirit descended upon him with the words, "This is my beloved Son with whom I am well pleased" (Matthew 3:17). Jesus went off into the desert, then, knowing that he was beloved of God. Wright continues:

> [Discernment] is not simply about resisting what is evil, self-absorbed, or destructive. It is about foundational identity. It is about who we know ourselves ultimately to be. It is about paying attention to the ways in which the limited power we wield, the modest respect we command, the taken-for-granted resources we hold provide us with our primary sense of meaning. To what extent do we "know" ourselves first as civic and church leaders, or as respectable citizens or conscientious parents or homeowners or degree holders or job holders and not at all as beloved

daughters and sons of God? We are beloved not because of what we do. We are beloved because we are.[3]

For some of us, believing that we are beloved just because we exist is difficult. Then discernment also becomes difficult, because we have no reason to think that God has much to say to us or that God cares what happens to us unless it is to judge us harshly for our faults. If that is true for you, let me encourage you to reconsider and to find resources or people who can help you examine and rethink your image of God and of God's desire for you. No matter how impossible it may seem, God loves each of us totally and unconditionally—no ifs, ands, or buts.

THE GIFTS OF SURRENDER

Another barrier to practicing discernment is the fear of surrendering our will to God's. *Surrender* is a dirty word in this culture; it is the equivalent of admitting you are weak and helpless. We like being in control, the captains of our own destiny. We want to be in charge of things, at least those things that intersect with our own world. The Horatio Alger myth is a powerful one in our culture. Pulling ourselves up by the bootstraps and making something of ourselves—not God making something of us—is to be admired. In some of the retreats I have led, people have struggled hard with the *Rule of Saint Benedict*—a sixth-century monastic book about living with God at the center of life. The book feels intensely authoritarian to those who aren't familiar with the context in which it was written and who haven't studied the book in its entirety. But I know, from my own experience of reading it years ago versus reading it now, that it is the idea of turning over control of one's life to *anyone* that distresses people who are new to the spiritual life; it isn't the specific instructions Benedict gives. Control and power are aphrodisiacs in our culture; surrender is for losers.

Surrendering also implies turning over our will completely to God once and for all and never having to do so again. It seems like an all-or-nothing proposition. Ultimately, however, surrender is a gift of God and not something that is totally within our control. None of us commit ourselves to God once and for all; we do so over and over throughout our lives. The process of aligning our will with God's will is gradual, brought about through our deepening love of God, our growing ability to pay attention, and, finally, our desire to live as God has called us to do. Rueben Job, a retired bishop in the United Methodist Church, describes the process this way:

> Practicing preference for God has always been the first commandment and the first step toward faithful living. From this stance we seek God and God's companionship first. And as we do so, we learn to surrender our will to God's will. We will learn that God's presence and direction can be trusted. From this vantage point we learn that God's will is good and to be desired. When these truths begin to become a part of our very lives, discernment becomes a natural consequence of our daily walk with God.[4]

We do not need to give up, or surrender, our dreams and deepest desires in order to commit ourselves to living God's way; God speaks to our heart through those very desires. All of this points to the difficulty of the word *surrender*. For women particularly but also for many men, the idea of surrendering ourselves can be dangerous and a barrier to our having a full relationship with God. Perhaps a better way to think of the process of bringing our own desires and God's desires into better alignment is to think of it as accepting God's invitation to partner with us. As we learn to listen to God more fully (to practice a preference for God, as Rueben Job states) and as our love for God deepens, our own dreams and desires naturally move closer to those God has for us.

Think of the process of surrendering to or partnering with God as you would a car getting onto the freeway. To get onto the freeway requires a certain resoluteness on our part. It is a deliberate act. Once on the freeway, we have to drive steadily and purposefully so that we stay on the road. At the same time, at least for experienced drivers, merging onto the freeway, switching lanes, and exiting are natural, almost automatic acts. They are hard the first few times you do them, but

Almighty God, in whom we live and move and have our being, you have made us for yourself, so that our hearts are restless till they rest in you; grant us purity of heart and strength of purpose, that no passion may hinder us from knowing your will, no weakness from doing it; but in your light may we see clearly, and in your service find perfect freedom; through Jesus Christ our Lord. Amen.

AUGUSTINE OF HIPPO

after that they come easily. The same principles apply as we grow spiritually. We "go with the flow" of traffic more often—we hear with the heart and discern God's will—almost without thinking about it, without engaging our will very consciously.

This partnering with God, at first, requires attention, practice, and commitment on our part. We cannot will that partnership any more than we can will ourselves to fall in love with someone. We may experience a sudden change of heart, a vision, or a moment of conversion in our life; these are important events. But absorbing the meaning of these peak moments and bringing them into our everyday lives takes time and patience. At some point, however, surrendering to God becomes natural, easy—something we desire with all our heart.

> *Ah, Lord, to whom all hearts are open, you can pilot the ship of our souls far better than we can. Stand up, Lord, and command the stormy wind and the troubled sea of our hearts to be still, and at peace in you, so that we may look up to you undisturbed, and rest in union with you, our Lord. Do not let us be carried hither and thither by wandering thoughts, but, forgetting all else, let us see and hear you alone. Renew our spirits; kindle in us your light, that it may shine within us, and our hearts may burn in love and adoration for you. Let your Holy Spirit dwell in us continually, and make us your temples and sanctuary. Fill us with divine love and light and life, with devout and heavenly thoughts, with comfort and strength, with joy and peace. Amen.*
>
> JOHANN ARNDT

LEAVING THE COMFORTS OF NORMAL

Whether we like our lives as they are right now or not, changing them is difficult. All of us have developed comfortable patterns and behaviors, often in childhood, that serve our needs. If that weren't true, we wouldn't have much use for all the New Year's resolutions we make each December or January. Most of us believe (or know) that a more regular prayer life, or a bit more exercise, or whatever else we resolve to change each year would be good for us, but we are so accustomed to working long hours, or coming home and switching on the tube or the stereo, or spending every evening out with friends, that we have trouble changing our habits to accommodate things that we wish were higher on the priority list—like God.

No doubt habits are hard to break. Maybe it's talking a lot to cover nervousness or staying very busy either to avoid contact with others or to avoid being alone. An early experience of deep disappointment or betrayal may have taught us to keep people at a comfortable distance so we won't get hurt again. These behaviors, even when they don't serve us very well as adults, are comfortable and familiar. Even when we know they prevent us from moving forward in life, these patterns and coping mechanisms feel safe and secure compared to new, unknown, and frightening possibilities. Even those who live in abusive environments—for example, the wife whose husband beats her—may have a hard time leaving because the environment is familiar. Having a husband and a relationship of any sort feels more familiar and seems safer than the unknown challenges of beginning a new life alone or living without financial security. Committing ourselves to live as

God desires, especially when it very possibly entails the disruption of familiar habits, can feel like placing all our future hopes on the spin of a roulette wheel.

Consider the story of Peter in Matthew 14. Jesus and the disciples have had a busy day. Jesus has spoken to the crowds, and about five thousand people have been fed. Jesus goes away alone for the night, but in the morning he comes walking across the water to the disciples, who are in a boat being battered by the waves of the sea. The story continues:

> Peter answered him, "Lord, if it is you, command me to come to you on the water." He said, "Come." So Peter got out of the boat, started walking on the water, and came toward Jesus. But when he noticed the strong wind, he became frightened, and beginning to sink, he cried out, "Lord, save me!" Jesus immediately reached out his hand and caught him, saying to him, "You of little faith, why did you doubt?" (Matthew 14:28–31)

In this story, the disciples have given up their lives to follow Jesus, and they are repeatedly confused by their new life. That they are in a boat being battered about by wild waves makes sense; this is a metaphor for what has happened to their lives. In the midst of all of this, Peter asks for some kind of assurance; he asks that Jesus prove himself by commanding Peter to do what Peter believes is impossible—to walk on the water. Jesus invites Peter to come to him, and for a moment Peter believes that all is possible, and he climbs out of the boat and walks toward Jesus. A few steps later, he realizes that what he is doing is unfamiliar and impossible, and fear causes him to start sinking. Jesus, more in kindness than anger, I think, invites Peter again into a new way of life and supports him in that; Peter is reassured.

This may ring true for those of us contemplating living differently. We have certain images of ourselves, expectations about what we can and cannot do, and understanding of how the world is structured. But at some point, something pulls us forward, crying, "Come." Maybe we make some progress in responding to the call; we get out of the boat and start walking on the water, like Peter, even though this activity is clearly outside of what we considered possible. We have heard the command, "come," with our heart, and the heart does not know what is impossible. Not long after this, the wind comes up and starts whipping the waves around again. We discover that we are in unfamiliar territory, and we become frightened. We long for the safety of the boat—our old way of being—as we begin to sink amidst the difficulties of our new life. It may take a great deal of courage to ask for

A Collect for Vocation in Daily Work

Almighty God our heavenly Father, you declare your glory and show forth your handiwork in the heavens and in the earth: Deliver us in our various occupations from the service of self alone, that we may do the work you give us to do in truth and beauty and for the common good; for the sake of him who came among us as one who serves, your Son Jesus Christ our Lord, who lives and reigns with you and the Holy Spirit, one God, for ever and ever. Amen.

THE BOOK OF COMMON PRAYER

help, to grip the hands and lines thrown out to us, and to continue on the path at this point.

Our stories need not be as dramatic as Peter's, though they may feel like it at times. One of the ways in which I feel called to respond to God is through writing and helping others deepen their spiritual lives, but I continue to wonder why God has chosen me for this task. I had no intention of writing, either as an avocation or a way to make a living. But a colleague of mine saw something in me and put opportunities in my path. My writing career then began with book reviews, moved on to feature articles, and finally developed into full-length books, much to my own surprise. And there are definitely times when I feel battered by the waves of balancing a demanding professional career with my love of writing. There are periods when the words flow easily, almost as if God were whispering them in my ear. At other times, the stress of trying to balance all the demands overwhelms me. I begin to sink, and I call, "Lord, save me," along with Peter. Through the years, I have learned that praying and writing are the same thing for me, and I value the connection I find to God when I am writing. At the same time, life was easier when I didn't have a "second" job!

If we are honest about discerning and living God's will, most of us probably hope that we will never be called to a life that asks us to change our own self-image, to give up whatever passes for safety and familiarity in our world, to live in a way that seems so entirely different from our own expectations. A friend of mine tells the story of leaving a corporate job in an industry in which he was well known and respected in order to work for himself. He had spent many years climbing to his high level of achievement and was clearly destined for success. Yet something was missing from his life. Working for the corporation was taxing, and he had very little time for the people and things he loved to do in his life. Even so, it took him more than a year to decide to leave the job and set himself up in business. The risks of being self-employed after years of an excellent salary and a good benefit package were intimidating, but he knew that God had called him to something more fulfilling. Once he got his own business started, he wondered why he'd ever delayed, but leaving a prestigious position and what passed for safety and comfort behind was hard to imagine in advance.

Willingness to give up self-image, as my friend did, even when it is not comfortable, and to launch out into the unknown requires courage and trust. Still, God's calls always bring with them great joy as well as tough choices and, sometimes, difficult moments. When my friend, for instance, gave up the security of his corporate job, he had no real way of knowing whether the money to pay the bills would come in. That was a brave decision on his part—one that probably entailed a few sleepless nights along the way.

Choosing to follow God's guidance for us may upset not only our individual world but wider worlds outside us. When we change, our families and circles of friends are forced to change, too. Whether they like it or not, friends, family, and colleagues must reevaluate or restructure their own behavior when we decide to act in a new way. That response may take the form of resistance or denial. My friend who left corporate life got lots of support and encouragement from those close to him but no support from some of his friends and colleagues, who felt he was acting foolishly. In reality, those who didn't support him may have been envious of his decision to do what his heart desired, what he discerned that God had called him to do. Perhaps they lacked the courage to take the step he took, and his strength threatened them. Rather than admit that, his former friends disparaged his decision and encouraged him not to rock the boat. Discernment of a new direction brings this risk with it sometimes. The fear and discomfort we may feel when we discern a change in direction for our own lives may well cause confusion and disorientation for others.

If, for instance, we have a high-powered position that brings with it high prestige and financial reward, what happens when we discern that our part in bringing about heaven on earth is to be a lower-paid schoolteacher instead? That is not to say there is a single thing wrong with being a schoolteacher; the profession is vastly underrated and underpaid. But that is precisely the difficulty for the person switching gears. The social circle in which he or she travels is likely to change, as is the standard of living. Perhaps the change of career involves going back to school for a couple of years or even moving to a new home or city. All of this might be acceptable and even exciting to the person who has a sense of God's call to teach, but family members, friends, and others may find the change significantly more difficult. Perhaps family members are accustomed to a high standard of living and will have to leave that behind. Friends who have been accustomed to talking about work all the time find few points of connection in the new scenario. Dealing with all of that can be very taxing. That's why a commitment to discerning God's guidance in our lives and acting on it requires not only courage but compassion—for ourselves and for others as well.

IGNORING THE WORLD'S IDOLS

Acting upon God's dreams for the world may also put us in conflict with those ideals our culture holds dear, for God's call is not usually to power, prestige, and wealth—the highest values in contemporary Western culture. Look, for instance, at the kinds of statements advertisers use to convince us to buy items and services. In a single issue of a national magazine, I found some of the following inducements for attaining power, prestige, and wealth:

- An ad stating that owning a wide-screen television means things are really getting better
- A software ad promising that the product will help you trounce your competition
- A car ad offering "the feel of refined power" and promising that the car "stimulates all your senses"
- An ad claiming that the use of a particular credit card guarantees access to the top airlines, hotels, and even the entire world
- An ad suggesting that by purchasing the company's services, you will finally be able to see yourself as successful
- An ad for an expensive hotel claiming to be your friend, where no favor was too big to ask
- An airline ad claiming you would earn status by being a member of their program

There were lots more ads, but you get the idea. We are surrounded by images of power, personal glory, and importance. After all, who needs God when you can have an international hotel as your friend? To choose to discern and act on God's desires may well mean that we choose to give up values the culture holds dear, just as Jesus did in the wilderness thousands of years ago.

That story of Jesus' experience of temptations in the wilderness is one of the classic stories of discernment. Jesus is led to the desert after his baptism, and he spends forty days and nights there fasting. At the end of this period he is hungry, and the tempter comes to Jesus with amazing demands and offers. "Just turn the stones into bread and be fed," the tempter says. Then the Devil suggests that Jesus throw himself off a high place to prove that he is the Son of God. God will surely save Jesus from any harm. Finally, the Devil offers Jesus all the riches and splendors in the world if Jesus will only worship the tempter. Jesus refuses each time and finally tells the Devil to be gone.

Wendy Wright offers a wonderful analysis of this story in her article on discernment. "Jesus recognizes for what they are the attractive, in fact very alluring, invitations to be able to procure what one hungers for, to be admired, even worshipped, and to own all imaginable goods," she writes. "They are suggestions from a spirit different from the one that compelled him into the desert in the first place. That first Spirit prompts him instead to refuse and as a consequence to embrace powerlessness, humility, and poverty. When he had embraced these, scripture relays, he was ministered to by angels."[5]

Maybe we won't be asked to embrace powerlessness, humility, and poverty as a result of discerning and living God's desires, though we never know. But we may discover that we are called to stop seeing ourselves as indispensable at work, as a person who can't take a sick day, who can't manage the workload without working sixty hours a week, or who is defined by what she buys and owns. Perhaps we will find that we really are a slave to something that separates us from God—work, alcohol, drugs, sex, shopping, "being right," or whatever—and we have to admit that we are powerless and ask God's help. Maybe we will discover that the wide-screen television, the chance to trounce our competition, and a hotel that claims to be our friend aren't all they are cracked up to be. Each of us has a temptation or two that hooks us easily. The risk of practicing discernment is that we will come face-to-face with them and have to stretch every fiber of our being to banish them, as Jesus did in the wilderness.

I have had to encounter this more than once in my own life. Anyone who knows me can tell you that I sometimes work too hard for too many hours, too intensely. I can be enormously single-minded about my work and forget all about the rest of my life. There are even times when I am so engrossed in "doing" instead of "being" that I forget to pay attention to the needs of those around me. I have been aware of this for a number of years and have spent many hours in spiritual direction looking at the reasons I am so easily hooked by work and trying to understand the spiritual consequences of that. But I had a hard time really understanding how this affected me and my relationship with God and all of creation until I realized one day that the tempter, for me, lives within my work life. This has nothing to do with the particular work or any specific employer I've

Lord God, almighty and everlasting Father, you have brought us in safety to this new day: Preserve us with your mighty power, that we may not fall into sin, nor be overcome by adversity; and in all we do, direct us to the fulfilling of your purpose; through Jesus Christ our Lord. Amen.

THE BOOK OF COMMON PRAYER

worked for. I am simply susceptible to the inducements of the tempter who tells me that people will admire me if I work hard, that I can be indispensable and, therefore, truly needed. My own time in prayer, in listening for God's will, however, tells me that the tempter is wrong. I am loved simply because I exist, not for how much I can accomplish in a given day. But even knowing that, some days I still struggle to resist what I have come to know as the voice of evil in my life—the voice that promises me all the riches in the world if I will just let work replace God as the center of my existence.

Save us from the time of trial, and deliver us from evil. For the kingdom, the power, and the glory are yours.

THE LORD'S PRAYER

To live with God at the center of our lives is what discernment is all about. It means we turn away from idolatry of the individual and self-sufficiency. The ads on our billboards, televisions, radios, and magazines tell the story again. The military tells us to "be all you can be." A health insurance company has a billboard that says, "It's all about you." Just yesterday, while waiting to get a haircut, I saw a larger-than-average-size issue of a national magazine, *The Power Issue,* in which every feature story was about someone powerful or about the most powerful clothes or makeup you could wear. Perhaps my favorite example of the confusion between individual control and power and what is truly important in our world came during a recent stay at a large hotel. In the drawer next to the bed were three books: the *Holy Bible,* the *Book of Mormon,* and a copy of the hotel chain owner's book on how to be successful in business. It is fashionable to make our jobs into the center of our world and work very hard to prove that we are absolutely indispensable, because we often believe it really *is* all about us.

Hearing with the Heart

A commitment to living as God desires requires that we put God, instead of ourselves, at the center. Doing that will not please many in the world around us, but it seems that it never has. The pressures of our own lives, personal histories, and cultural norms make it difficult to truly make a commitment to discerning and living God's will. Many of us can identify with the rich young man in the gospels who has led a good life and kept God's commandments but who somehow senses that there is more to the relationship with God than just keeping to the law. He comes to Jesus and asks, "Teacher, what good deed must I do to have eternal life?" (Matthew 19:16). Jesus' answer, after ascertaining that the young man has kept the commandments, is that he should go sell all that he owns, give it to the poor, and follow Jesus. The young man went away sorrowfully, as he owned a great deal and could not give it all up. Just as was true for this man, it is easier for many of us (and I include myself in this group) to follow the law—to keep rules and develop spiritual practices—than it is to truly fall in love with God, make God the center of our world, and follow that path without regard to power, prestige, and wealth.

The good news is that discernment is not just about sacrifice. Most of us will not be asked to give up everything we own and live a life of poverty. Discernment involves paying attention to God and to what the world needs from us, as well as to God in the form of our deepest desires. Frederick Buechner, a Presbyterian minister and a wonderful writer, talks about this when he speaks about discernment and the work we find to do:

> There are all different kinds of voices calling you to all different kinds of work, and the problem is to find out which is the voice of God rather than

of Society, say, or the Superego, of Self-Interest. By and large a good rule for finding this out is this: The kind of work God usually calls you to is the kind of work (a) that you need most to do and (b) that the world most needs to have done. . . . The place God calls you to is the place where your deep gladness and the world's deep hunger meet.[6]

The process of committing ourselves to God, however, cannot and does not happen all at once. Nor does God ask this of us; the invitation to follow will be issued over and over again throughout the course of our lives. God does not give up on us. Sometimes we discern that God calls us in a particular direction, but we can't respond at that time. Maybe we're just not ready, or perhaps a response on our part would inconvenience others at a level we're not prepared to accept right now. If we must walk away in sorrow today, perhaps we will be ready to follow next week or next year. We begin the journey, however, with some expression of willingness to learn to listen to God's desires more deeply, and we do that knowing that obstacles stand in our way, just as Anne Lamott's fear stood in her way on the beach and my work sometimes interferes with mine. Even so, we continue to try to listen for God. We pray and wait—patiently or otherwise—for the new ears and eyes that give us the ability to really see and

May the strength of God pilot us,
may the power of God preserve us,
may the wisdom of God instruct us,
may the hand of God protect us,
may the way of God direct us,
may the shield of God defend us,
may the host of God guard us
against the snares of evil
and the temptations of the world.

PATRICK

hear. And we resist, to the best of our ability, all the personal and cultural obstacles between us and what God desires for us.

To begin the journey along this path requires courage and compassion, for the way is unclear, and we don't know what we will find or what we may be asked to do along the way. "Beware all ye who enter here" should be posted at the entrance to the pathway. This is not the road to glory, fame, and riches, at least not as the world defines them. This is, however, the way to God and the riches of a life lived in God. The journey is not always an easy one, but, speaking from my own experience, it is worth the effort.

Part Two

TOOLS

FOR

DISCERNMENT

Consider the next few chapters to be your toolbox for everyday discernment. They are full of the real basics—the stuff you're going to want to keep handy for easy access. These tools will help you open up your heart so that it truly sees and hears. The kinds of prayer we'll explore here will help you attune yourself to the sound of God's voice. Practicing the art of reading your own life will help you see how God has guided you in the past so you can better recognize what God desires for your future. Studying what others have discovered about God's vision for all of creation provides a context for testing and confirming your own understanding of God's guidance, as will conversation with soul friends and others who walk the spiritual path alongside you.

There's nothing particularly flashy or spectacular here—no advanced degrees needed for you to understand. But without some experience with these foundational tools as a part of your everyday life, you'll probably have a hard time discerning God's will at a major transition or crisis point in your life. Theodore of Pherme, an ancient monk and Desert Father, tells the story of a young monk who visited him, speaking about all sorts of things he had never practiced. Theodore's response to the young monk is quite simple: "You have not yet found a ship nor put your cargo aboard and before you have sailed, you have already arrived at the city. Do the work first; then you will have the speed you are making now."[1] Think of these skills as ones that "prepare your ship to sail." They will help you build a solid relationship with God, as well as a clearer sense of God's guidance in your life. That way, when it's time for a real heart-to-heart conversation about something important, you'll already know how to talk with God and have some confidence in the guidance you receive.

Chapter Three

THE PRAYERFUL HEART

If we take the Eucharist once a year, take no time to be apart and to listen for the Voice, give God some directives and pointers for five minutes a day and call it prayer, and do none of the things that the faithful who traveled this road before us would remind us to do, then we are likely to only talk to God and never hear a response.[1]

ROBERT BENSON

We all pray whether we think of it as praying or not," says Frederick Buechner.[2] The "or not" in Buechner's sentence is important, because so often we limit our ideas about what prayer is or is not, and by doing that we limit our relationship with God. Prayer sounds mysterious and mystical to some people; for others it is the rote recitation of established prayers—something they say because they think they should or because they have

Great Shepherd of thy people, hear,
Thy presence now display;
As thou hast given a place for prayer,
So give us heart to pray.

always done it that way. Prayer is mysterious but not in the sense of being magical or in some superstitious way of ensuring that God does what you want. Praying is simply conversation or contact with God—nothing more and nothing less. And regular contact with God is a cornerstone for developing the hearing heart and using it for discernment.

Think of prayer as the child's game of peekaboo. A dad covers his own face with his hands and asks, "Where's Daddy?" or "Where's Suzie?" Finally, he takes his hands from his face and hollers, "Peekaboo!" Prayer is one of the tools we use to help us remove our hands from our face (it is never God hiding) so we can be in contact with God. In the busyness of the everyday, we hide our face—and our souls—with our hands. But in prayer we move them and reveal ourselves. We think that God will be surprised by what God sees, and it takes a lifetime to find out that this is not so. God delights in those moments, just as the child delights in seeing its parent's face again.

Another way to imagine the practice of prayer is to think of it as a conversation. We meet God in prayer for the same reasons we would meet a good friend for dinner. It is good to see one another, to catch up on what's going on in our lives, to share a personal struggle, to be with someone we care about and who cares about us. It isn't that God doesn't know what is on our hearts and minds when we fail to pray, but we'll have no idea what God "thinks" of all of that if we don't bother to ask for and listen to the response.

Praying—being present to God—is one of the ways we come to know God's voice with the eyes and ears of our hearts. Just as you come to know a friend's life story, hopes, and desires through time spent together listening and caring, so we come to know God's story and develop a sense of God's deepest desires. In *Living Prayer*, contemporary author Robert Benson talks about learning to pray by sitting alone in a church sanctuary with silence and books as his only companions:

> I began to learn to be comfortable with the silence itself, and to come to see it as presence rather than as absence. I began to let my mind wander aimlessly until it came to rest, and later to detach myself from the places where it had wandered so that it might rest in the Presence. I began to learn to pray with a pen in my hand, scribbling in a journal the scraps and fragments of prayer and remembrance and story and recollection that came to me. I began to read the psalms in a regular pattern that brought them around again and again, until they began to reveal their mysterious power to become the prayer of my heart on the days when I would not have been able to find my own words to describe or express the joy or wonder or despair or fear that was inside of me.[3]

Benson speaks of this time spent learning to pray as a kind of correspondence course in prayer. He discovered what we all do eventually: learning to listen actively for God's dream and guidance takes practice. Praying only during the stressful moments of our lives is like an ice-skater hitting the ice for the first time the week before a major competition. Ice-skaters who consistently skate well do so because they have spent many hours on the ice practicing their jumps, spins, and other moves. When the stressful competition arrives, they can count on their bodies knowing the routine and the timing so well that not even crowds of people and immense pressure confuse them. So it is with prayer. Through a regular practice, we come to know God's part and voice in prayer and in our life as a whole. And we have a better chance of recognizing God's guidance, not confusing it with the voices of our own ego or of the culture around us in more stressful moments.

There are probably as many ways to pray as there are people in this world. Each of us has a different relationship with God, so each of us finds that some ways of praying further that relationship better than others. In Part Three, we'll look at some specific ways of praying that may aid in discernment about a particular concern, but these will be easier if you are already in the habit of including the practices of silence and listening in your regular prayer life. Three specific prayer practices will help us listen more deeply for God's voice: being silent, practicing openness to guidance in prayer, and using the prayer of *Examen*.

LISTENING TO THE SILENCE

Most people really dislike silence. I've known city people who have gone to stay in the country and found they couldn't sleep because it was too quiet. In part, we are simply accustomed to noise and are rarely in a truly quiet place. We hear our computers whirring, cars driving by, the phone and doorbell ringing, the neighbors playing the stereo too loud, others in the house or office talking on the phone. These are signs of business, productivity, and life. We are habituated to noise, without even knowing it, and silence unnerves us. It disturbs us particularly when we are with others. Abba Theopilus, Archbishop of Alexandria in the fifth century, went out into the desert to hear the wisdom of Abba Pambo one day and was met with silence. "Say something to the archbishop, so that he may be edified," the gathered brethren say, as the story continues. Abba Pambo's response was quite simple: "If he is not edified by my silence, he will not be edified by my speech."[4]

Be still and know that I am God.

PSALM 46:10

Silence feels empty and uncomfortable to most of us, particularly when we are new to the practice. We avoid lulls in the conversation, even when we have permission to be quiet. I have been on weekend retreats where the leader sug-

For God alone my soul waits in silence.

PSALM 62:1

gested short periods of silence—twenty minutes or so—and people were simply unable to sustain that. Conversations broke out within minutes because people were so uncomfortable with having nothing to do or say, even for a short period of time.

For others silence is frightening. When the noise around us stops, we are left with our own thoughts and, perhaps, our fears and worries. One of my favorite contemporary monastic "handbooks" recognizes how difficult silence can be: "Silence is a constant source of restoration. Yet its healing power does not come cheaply. It depends on our willingness to face all that is within us, light and dark, and to heed all the inner voices that make themselves heard in silence."[5]

But we must befriend silence if we are to practice discernment, because silence lets us hear God's part in the conversation. Have you ever been around a couple who have lived together for many years—two people who are very comfortable with one another? They can sit in a room together in perfectly companionable silence. They don't need to use words all the time to communicate with each other. Even in silence there is a strong bond between them that is almost palpable. That's what being silent with God is like.

When we need to talk all the time or have noise as a part of our every waking minute, we may not be able to hear the voice of God over the din. Perhaps you've

Let the words of my mouth and the meditation of my heart be acceptable to you, O LORD, my rock and my redeemer.

PSALM 19:14

been part of a conversation with someone else who simply won't stop talking. It doesn't take long to get bored when you're on the receiving end of a one-sided conversation. Although God may not get bored when you dominate the conversation, you won't be able to hear anything God has to say, should God manage to get a word in edgewise.

Have you ever noticed how often, as reported in the gospels, Jesus went off alone to be quiet? Aside from the forty days in the wilderness following his baptism, Jesus regularly left the crowds behind to pray in solitude and, presumably, in silence. (See Matthew 14:23, Mark 1:35, Mark 6:45–46, Luke 4:42, and John 6:15.) The crowds thought this was as odd as we think our silence is today. They kept finding Jesus and dragging him back to the activity at hand, but Jesus kept trying to find some moments of solitude. The "crowds" often come and drag us away from our quiet, too. Like Jesus, however, we must be prepared to insist on some silence where we can pray and listen for God.

Hearing with the Heart

If silence is a new practice for you, try the following:

1. Find a place where you can sit undisturbed by phones, people, television, or music for a little while.

2. Find a comfortable position in which to sit. Many people find it best to sit in a chair or against something that supports the back. Make sure that your legs are uncrossed and there are no cramped body parts to cut off your circulation if you are still for a while.

3. Depending on the room temperature, you may even want to have a blanket over your legs; when we sit still for a while, our body temperature drops a little, and being cold will be a distraction and hindrance to silent prayer.

4. Use your watch or a timer, especially if you are new to sitting in silence. Set it for just five minutes at first. I guarantee you that five minutes will seem like a long time at the beginning.

5. Relax and breathe deeply for a few moments. Try to notice any tension in your body—neck, stomach, legs, or elsewhere—and release it to the best of your ability.

6. Try to clear your mind of the day's events, the decisions you need to make, the things you need to do next, or whatever else is on your mind.

If you are like most people, you will find all this very difficult. In Mark Salzman's recent novel *Lying Awake,* the main character is trying to empty her mind of "all that was not God, but found that it was like trying to empty an ocean: where do you put the water?"[6] Sometimes it helps to breathe deeply and focus on your breath or even count your breaths. Others find that focusing on a sacred word (*shalom, God, peace, love*) or phrase (My soul waits for the Lord) can be helpful. Physical objects such as candles or an image in the mind can focus attention. I find it particularly useful to imagine placing all the things that are floating around in my thoughts on a table and carefully moving them to the side so that I clear the table top.

Find whatever works best for you, but remember to be gentle with yourself when your thoughts keep intruding on the silence. Being angry and harsh with the concerns that disturb your silence will only defeat the purpose of quiet, contemplative time.

If an image or suggestion comes to mind (other than one about getting back to the things on your to-do list), pay attention to it. Notice, too, whatever feelings you have about what you are sensing. What wisdom might that image or suggestion have for you?

Finally, wait expectantly for a sense of God's presence, but don't be surprised or distressed if "nothing happens." God is present, whether we recognize that or not, and sometimes we simply sit with God in companionable silence.

It takes practice to learn to silence the clatter of our thoughts. At first it feels as if you're standing on a busy street corner in Manhattan trying to banish the taxi horns, the buses, the passers-by on their cell phones. Silence seems like an impossibility. Over time, however, if you make a space for it regularly, you will find that it is possible to sit in relative silence for extended periods of time—twenty to thirty minutes or more. That, in turn, creates a space, free of other noises, in which God's guidance can be sought and heard in the heart.

But what of those times when silence is simply emptiness rather than a feeling of communication? For all of us, there are times when silence is just silence, when we feel like we're communing with an absent God rather than a dear friend. But the fact that we have no sense of God's presence does not mean that God is absent or that nothing is happening. Even though there are no spiritual guarantees, these dry or silent spaces are often the prelude to growth. "Even if you don't believe anybody's listening," says Frederick Buechner, "at least you'll be listening."[7] In the very next sentence, however, Buechner reminds us to believe that Someone is listening. God is always present and listening whether we feel God's presence or not. Think of your silent presence as being sufficient, just as you would continue to be present to a friend even when the relationship feels rocky. "There will be days when [prayer] is a burden to you," says *The Rule of Taizé,* a handbook for spiritual living and guidance originally written for the popular ecumenical religious community in the south of France. "On such occasions know how to offer your body, since your presence itself already signifies your desire, momentarily unrealizable, to praise your Lord."[8]

THY WILL BE DONE

Silence in prayer also helps us drop our agendas—our to-do lists—for God. Even though it's common and perfectly acceptable to come to God in prayer with a concern and a proposed solution, openness to God's will is more the attitude to cultivate as part of discernment. And that requires admitting that we don't always know what God's will is. Another story from the Desert Fathers illustrates the wisdom of using some of the words we least like to say: "I don't know."

One day some old men came to see Abba Anthony. In the midst of them was Abba Joseph. Wanting to test them, the old man suggested a text from the Scriptures, and, beginning with the youngest, he asked them what it meant. Each gave his opinion as he was able. But to each one the old man said, "You have not understood it." Last of all he said to Abba Joseph, "How would you explain this saying?" and he replied, "I do not know." Then Abba Anthony said, "Indeed, Abba Joseph has found the way, for he has said: 'I do not know.'"[9]

It is a natural human tendency to come to God saying something like, "Dear God, I've been offered this wonderful new job. I think I should take it. Don't you?" We expect to hear resounding agreement to a question stated like that, and we often close our ears to anything that sounds like no. But in discernment, we come before God with a hearing heart and say that we are faced with a new opportunity; we ask if this is consistent with God's desires. And then we wait, with both expectancy and patience, for guidance. Or at least we try.

If you grew up in a church tradition, you may not have much experience with letting go of the "please God do this" list. Many churches include a time of intercessory prayers—prayers for others—in their worship services, and the requests are usually specific. They include prayers for healing, wisdom, comfort, and so on. That is just as it should be, and you don't need to abandon those prayers. But if we wish to know what God desires rather than what we think should happen, we need to spend at least some of our prayer time holding the world and our specific concerns before God without an agenda, knowing that God knows what is needed better than we do.

A few years ago, I was a member of a small prayer group that met monthly to pass on prayer requests received from others. In relaying these requests, some of the group's members revealed an enormous amount of detail about the person requesting prayers, and they were very specific about what we should be asking of God. There were discussions within the group about whether we really needed to know all the details of other people's private lives or whether a simple request for our prayers for someone was enough. While some people felt that the detail and specific requests were helpful, many of us sensed that God already knew the details of people's lives and that only God knew the true need of the person requesting prayer. It was one thing to remember people in our prayers, to add our healing and transforming energies to God's; it was another thing entirely to try to tell God what to do.

> *Thy Kingdom come,*
> *Thy will be done on earth*
> *as it is in heaven.*
>
> THE LORD'S PRAYER

It is the same when we are trying to discern God's will for our own lives. All too often, we have a plan of our own—one that may or may not match God's hope for us. Like the monks described earlier, we boldly interpret God's words for ourselves without stopping to think that we might be wrong. Sometimes the wiser response is to continue listening with our hearts and say, "I don't know," at least for the moment. By doing this, we let God be God; we then add our energy and desires to God's rather than ask God to do it our way instead.

One way of practicing openness to God's will in prayer is to simply hold mental images of those you are concerned about in God's light without asking for anything. Try this:

1. As with practicing silence, find a place where you can pray without being disturbed for five to thirty minutes. Make sure the room's temperature is reasonable, and sit in a comfortable position that supports your back and allows for free circulation of your bloodstream.

2. Take a few deep breaths and focus on relaxing your body, letting go of whatever to-do lists or other concerns you have on your mind.

3. Find an image of God's love that works for you. That might be picturing God's love as a bright light, or as God's hand open and waiting to receive your concerns, or as anything else that suggests God's receptivity to you.

4. Without asking for anything, name the people or the situations that you wish to hold before God, and imagine them being held in God's loving presence. You might see them wrapped in bright light, for instance, or being cradled in God's hand. Hold them there for as long as you wish, and then move on to the next person or situation you wish to place before God.

5. Include all sorts of people and events in this exercise: individuals who are in need of help, your own needs, countries where people are at war or starving, political situations, those suffering after a natural disaster, and even those who are experiencing great joys.

6. Conclude with a brief prayer of gratitude for God's loving presence in all these situations.

This practice may feel odd to you at first, particularly if you are used to asking God for specific solutions or actions for the people and things that concern you. You don't have to give up doing that, but a regular practice of openness in prayer will help you give up the desire to control God's actions and make you more open to God's guidance in your own life and for the world.

If you find this practice difficult or if you are practicing silence in order to listen to God's desires more completely, you might find a prayer service helpful. I have compiled one using biblical passages and prayers specifically focused on the issue of discernment in your life. You'll find that service in the Resource section. It can be prayed by yourself or with a group of others who are also trying to open their hearts to discernment. But, as with our other prayer practices, be sure to leave lots of time for silent reflection during the service. Appropriate places for silent meditation are marked in the service itself.

> *Lord, what particulars we pray for, we know not, we dare not, we humbly tender a blank into the hands of Almighty God; write therein, Lord, what thou wilt, where thou wilt, by whom thou wilt.*
>
> THOMAS FULLER

SEEING WITH THE HEART

A little fish was swimming around in the ocean, when he came across an older (and presumably wiser) fish.

> "Excuse me," said the little fish. "You are older than I, so can you tell me where to find this thing they call the ocean?"
>
> "The ocean," said the older fish, "is the thing you are in now."
>
> "Oh, this? But this is water. What I'm seeking is the ocean," said the disappointed fish as he swam away to search elsewhere.[10]

We are often just like that little fish. As odd as it may sound, we're not always aware of or paying attention to the changes in our listening practices that occur over time so we can incorporate that into our daily life. Sometimes we don't realize that we are already swimming in the ocean, and if we don't know that the water around us is the ocean, we're going to waste a lot of time seeking what we've already found. Put another way, it is easier to be aware of the ways in which we are not paying attention to and following God's guidance than to focus on those times when we have been alert and responsive. Particularly when we've been raised on the image of an angry or punishing God, it is too easy to pay attention to our shortcomings and inabilities instead of taking delight in those moments when we have drawn closer to God.

The Prayer of *Examen,* or the Examination of Conscience, an ancient spiritual practice, helps us pay attention to our proximity to and our distance from God and God's desires for us. And despite the use of the word *examination,* the practice is intended as one to encourage and help us look within and learn to recognize God's guidance, not grade or punish us. One of the benefits of using this prayer regularly is that, over time, you will find yourself becoming increasingly aware of God's presence in the moment instead of hours or days later. When I was first learning to pay attention to my own angry feelings, for instance, I tended not to notice them for hours after the incident that brought them on. As I learned to fear my own anger less and pay more attention to my feelings in the moment, I began responding to anger more quickly rather than expe-

My prayer is to you, O LORD. At an acceptable time, O God, in the abundance of your steadfast love, answer me.

PSALM 69:13

Hearing with the Heart

riencing long time delays. The Prayer of *Examen* can help you do the same thing as you learn to notice God's presence and will in your life. By using it regularly, you'll gain the experience you need to be aware of God's presence in the moment instead of an hour, a day, or a week later. That, in turn, will help you discern God's guidance as you go through the day and respond accordingly.

Most faith traditions have some version of this kind of prayer that is used to review one's relationship with God. For the purposes of discernment, the Prayer of *Examen* can be used to help us pay attention to those moments in a day, week, or other time period in which we feel we have been in touch with and followed God's guidance and when the opposite has been true.

1. Find a place where you can be quiet for five to thirty minutes, and prepare yourself as described in the previous section on practicing silence.

2. Assume a comfortable position, and try to clear your mind of the day's concerns.

3. After a brief period of silence, begin by looking back over the day (or week or whatever other time period you have selected) and notice those times when you felt you were moving toward God's will for your life.

4. If you wish, you can make note of your thoughts in a journal. You may find it helpful to note some of the details of these times or activities as well. How did you feel during those times when you were trying to respond to God's guidance? Did God feel present to you at these moments? If so, how?

5. When you are ready, turn your attention to the second part of the prayer and review those moments when you were moving away from God's guidance. What feelings arise when you consider these memories? Spend some time thinking or writing about why you find it hard to accept God's guidance in some areas. Did you avoid doing what you are called to do out of fear or out of woundedness from previous life experience, anger, or other emotions?

6. You may find it helpful to pray for forgiveness or for healing, as appropriate, at the end of this time.

7. After considering both of these questions, resume your silence and try to listen for God's response to you. Close your session with a prayer of thanks for this time with God.

I find it helpful to do this practice at the end of the day while my memories of what has happened throughout the day and evening are fresh. If a daily schedule for this prayer is too difficult for you, you might try it at the end of the week, perhaps on the Sabbath. But some regular practice of the Prayer of *Examen* will help you become more aware of God's guidance and of your own responses.

Teach us to pray often,
that we may pray oftener.

JEREMY TAYLOR

All of these prayer practices—silence, openness, and *Examen*—help open your heart to a greater awareness of the presence of God and to the development of the new eyes, ears, and heart we need for the practice of discernment. They are the conversational tools you need in order to know God better. You do not need to make space for all of these every day. Some will be useful on a regular basis; you might find others helpful on a more occasional basis. Find your own rhythm and style for nurturing openness in prayer, and the timetables that work best for you. What matters most is not how, when, and where you find spaces for silence and openness to God but only that you nurture those spaces as they open your heart and help it to hear.

Chapter Four

THE ATTENTIVE HEART

Discernment requires that we pay attention. . . . [It] is about feeling texture, assessing weight, watching the plumb line, listening for overtones, searching for shards, feeling the quickening, surrendering to love.[1]

WENDY WRIGHT

In *Let Your Life Speak,* a wonderful book on vocation, when Parker Palmer looked back at some episodes of depression in his life, he discovered that the malady was trying to tell him something. After years of ignoring what his life was trying—gently at first and then more forcefully—to tell him, depression finally got him to pay attention to what God was calling him to be.[2] Palmer is not alone in neglecting to pay attention to the clues God leaves us throughout our lives. Too often we wait for God to appear in a burning bush or a whirlwind. We have been conditioned to think God will approach us in some highly dramatic way, as Cecil B. DeMille might have portrayed it in his epic film *The Ten Commandments.*

But God is usually subtler than that. Because God doesn't send e-mails or leave us detailed operating instructions for our lives, we need to learn to read our lives for clues that help us discern God's desires for us. Just as detectives solve mysteries by paying close attention to the details of a case, we too can discover God's hope for us by observing the details of our lives. By being aware of the gifts God has given us and the pattern of our lives, by listening to our dreams and the wisdom of our bodies, we can discern the unique self that God has created in each one of us and begin living more fully in God's presence. Reading and understanding the clues of our daily lives also helps us prepare to discern directions and make decisions that are consistent with God's guidance when we face major life decisions.

Pay attention, come to me;
listen and your soul will live.

ISAIAH 55:3 (JERUSALEM BIBLE)

DISCOVERING YOUR GIFTS

One day, my spiritual director asked me to do something that stopped me in my tracks. She asked me to list my gifts. Had I been asked to list my faults, I could have answered quickly, at length. But I was astonished to discover that after forty-some years of living, I was unable to name my gifts quickly. I should not have been all that surprised. Many of us go through major portions of our lives—maybe even our entire lives—without being asked to name our gifts. To be even remotely aware of them feels a bit prideful or un-Christian. But to know and name our gifts clues us in to God's desires for us as individuals. We have each been given particular gifts to help us fulfill our part in bringing about heaven on earth, and if we don't pay attention to that, we may spend a lot of time and energy trying to be someone other than who God calls us to be.

I learned this lesson the hard way many years ago. I lived in Berkeley, California, at the time, where the temperate weather conditions make a large homeless population possible. For several years, I tried working in soup kitchens and shelters, but I found the work difficult and frustrating and finally gave up trying to force myself to work with the homeless. I decided that my best way of helping the homeless was to give money to the organizations that were skilled in meeting their needs. One Sunday, a friend preached a sermon on helping the poor and feeding the hungry, and a major case of the "guilts" set in. After the service, I confessed my frustration about being so inept at working with the homeless, and I will never forget his response: "So you think God gave you the wrong gifts?"

My friend was well aware of my gifts in other areas and was gently suggesting that I pay attention to the gifts I had rather than those I did not. I had fallen into the trap of thinking I should have all gifts, be everything to everyone. But we are

Now we have received not the spirit of the world, but the Spirit that is from God, so that we may understand the gifts bestowed on us by God.

1 CORINTHIANS 2:12

Each has a particular gift from God, one having one kind and another a different kind.

1 CORINTHIANS 7:7B

not given gifts for our own glory so that the world will think of us as the most talented, brightest, most creative people around. We are each given specific gifts that help bring about God's kingdom on earth in our own unique way. You get some gifts; I get some others, and my next-door neighbors get their share, too. Paul writes in 1 Corinthians 12:7–11:

> To each is given the manifestation of the Spirit for the common good. . . .
> To one is given through the Spirit the utterance of wisdom, and to
> another the utterance of knowledge according to the same Spirit,
> to another faith by the same Spirit, to another gifts of healing by the
> one Spirit, to another the working of miracles, to another prophecy,
> to another the discernment of spirits, to another various kinds of tongues,
> to another the interpretation of tongues. *All these are activated by one
> and the same Spirit, who allots to each one individually just as the Spirit
> chooses* [emphasis added].

Paul's last line is particularly important. Each of us—every single one of us—receives gifts from the Spirit. It is so easy to look at other people and see them as gifted individuals yet be blind to our own gifts. But awareness of the gifts God has given us—and the ones that are not ours—helps us discern the right choices and the right paths.

Let each of you lead the life that the Lord has assigned, to which God called you.

1 CORINTHIANS 7:17

Maybe you've had a dream that seems to be quite common. Flora Wuellner, a gifted spiritual writer and teacher, speaks of it in her book *Prayer, Fear, and Our Powers.* Every time she mentions this dream in class, she writes, students nod their heads in recognition.[3] The dream has many variations, but the gist of it is that the dreamer finds herself at the end of a semester in school and suddenly realizes that she signed up for a class that she forgot to attend all semester. (It was a French class, in my case.) Not only is the dreamer panicked about the failing grade that she is about to receive, but she experiences distress that she "forgot" all about something that was once important to her. This dream, Wuellner asserts, is about "our major purpose in life, our unique gift to the world which we were born to share but which most of us have either forgotten or have never even discerned."[4]

Just as the detective who misreads a clue goes down the wrong path in solving a mystery, when we ignore, forget, or fail to discern our gifts, we lack information we need for discerning wisely. Until we can name our gifts clearly, we may keep taking the wrong jobs, finding ourselves in the wrong relationships, and going down other paths that are not meant for us. If you don't know that you are gifted in fostering relationships, for example, and you take a job crunching numbers all day instead, you will likely end up being angry, frustrated, bored, and tired at the end of the day. This isn't what God hopes for each of us. God has given us our own unique gifts in order that we participate in the world in a way that is rich and fulfilling, not only for us but for the common good.

Do not neglect the gift that is in you.

1 TIMOTHY 4:14

Now we have received not the spirit of the world, but the Spirit that is from God, so that we may understand the gifts bestowed on us by God.

1 CORINTHIANS 2:12

NAMING YOUR GIFTS

The closest many of us have come to naming our gifts was probably in the process of looking for a job. Career counselors focus on what they call transferable skills—the things we do well in one arena that could help us in another. Counselors also ask you to list the things that you enjoy doing or have done well in the past as part of defining what you would like to do in the future. Even if you have never sought help in thinking about career possibilities, you have probably written a résumé or curriculum vitae that requires you to list your past accomplishments and skills in a way that convinces others of your future capabilities.

All these things relate to the term *gifts* as I use it here. Gifts are those abilities that seem to arise from within you without any training or conscious development. Perhaps they are even inborn. Using them energizes us, feeds us at some deep level. A friend of mine tells a story about a nun attached to a religious order devoted to teaching. For many years, this young woman taught school children, but she didn't find much joy in the work. One day, while organizing a benefit event for the local poor, she discovered that her real gift was working with those who were poor. That work was effortless and brought her great joy in a way that teaching had never done. She discovered what many of us do at one time or another: work we do because we ought to or because of other people's expectations brings little joy to ourselves or to others. She switched religious orders soon after that in order to use the gifts God had given her rather than continue to engage in a ministry that was never really hers.

Hearing with the Heart

That story highlights the difference between our gifts and our skills. On the one hand, using our natural or inborn gifts—whatever they may be—engages our joy, creativity, and energy. Skills, on the other hand, are learned and deliberately developed. Skills, like gifts, can be absolutely anything; one person's skill could be another person's gift. I have learned to be competent at budgeting, for instance, but it certainly wasn't an innate gift of mine. Living that primarily uses skills wears us out much of the time. Our inner resources get drained when we exercise skills too often; continuing to use skills primarily empties our internal reservoirs. We are like the nun who was worn out by teaching because, although she was skilled as an instructor, teaching was not her gift.

When we use our gifts more than our skills, we feel alive and energized. The inner resources seem boundless and constantly refilled rather than depleted. Parker Palmer, using different words, talks about the same thing in *Let Your Life Speak*. As a university faculty member and as an administrator, he was competent, well respected, and very unhappy. He was using his skills in prestigious settings, but they brought him little joy. When he started to pay attention to what he really wanted to do, to his real gifts of teaching outside of institutional settings, he began to flourish again.

Charles Bryant, who conducts workshops to help people identify their spiritual gifts, says that when we use those gifts we may "wear out but will never burn out."[5] That's because in using our gifts we are following God's call. We gratefully use the gifts, given us by God, to be who we are called to be; we don't try to be something we are not.

WHAT ARE YOUR GIFTS?

So what are your gifts? Perhaps you have already spent some time thinking about your gifts and can make a list of them right now. But if you find this as difficult as I did, let me suggest some strategies for uncovering your God-given gifts. First, try to separate your gifts from your skills.

List Your Gifts

Make a list of the things you love to do. Think back over the course of your whole life as you make this list, beginning with childhood. Many of us found great joy in a childhood activity, which we have ignored in our adult years, but remembering these activities may give you some clues about your gifts.

Look back through your life and make a list of the accomplishments, activities, jobs, hobbies, and relationships that have brought joy into your life. Look especially for times when these things brought with them an abundance of energy and enthusiasm. What gifts came with those activities or relationships? Did you have a wonderful summer at a youth camp teaching kids to swim? Perhaps you have the gift of teaching, leading, or mentoring. Do you enjoy feeding the homeless at the local food bank? Maybe one of your gifts is compassion. Are you the person everyone turns to when they can't figure out how to set up a new system or solve a problem? Then perhaps organization is your gift.

Now make as long a list as you can of things that have brought joy and energy into your life, and try to match each of these up with one or more gifts. If you find the same gifts emerging from many of your activities and relationships, that will give you a clue about where your strengths lie.

List Your Skills

Make a second list of things you do that don't seem to engage you at any deep level—that you can do without thinking much about them. They may be activities at which you excel, but they don't "light your fire" in any way. You may even actively dislike them, or doing them may leave you angry, bored, or fatigued. These are your skills.

Name Your Gifts

The list of skills can be put aside for now. What you are really seeking to name are your gifts. If your list of gifts is small or seems incomplete, try some of the steps that follow in order to gain a better sense of them.

ASK OTHERS Pick some close friends or confidantes and quiz them about their perception of your gifts. When I did this, I was amazed to discover that others could quickly identify gifts that I hadn't put on my list. Some of the things they mentioned were ones I should have thought of myself; others surprised me and provided food for thought. I remember, for instance, when I was considering leaving the bookstore business to take a job as an editor and found myself deeply conflicted over the move. A friend of mine commented that, as a bookseller, I had always focused on the content of books—a gift that might naturally lead one to become an editor. Once she said that, I wondered why I hadn't thought of it myself. It seemed obvious at the time, but it took someone else to point out that gift to me.

LOOK AT YOURSELF Look at the things you don't like about yourself. This probably sounds like an odd suggestion, but I found that by looking at the things I really dislike about myself (which is often called our shadow or dark side), I could find my gifts on the flip side. Although most of us aspire to being perfectly balanced human beings, this never happens. If we are one way, that probably means we are not another, contradictory, way. If we are impatient with people who don't learn quickly, our gift may be that we are very quick to assess and understand things. That doesn't excuse us from being compassionate to people who think at a different speed; each of us has different gifts, as 1 Corinthians reminds us. But the goal of this exercise is to use our ineptness, inaptitude, dislikes, and failures as clues to the gifts that may well lie on the other side of them rather than to rationalize or excuse what we dislike about ourselves.

Now that you have a list of your gifts, look at how you spend your days at work, in volunteer activities, and in leisure time. How much of your time is spent using your gifts and how much in using your skills? No one can spend 100 percent of his or her time using gifts alone; we all use a combination of gifts and skills. But if you find that 90 percent of your time is spent using your skills rather than your gifts, it may be time to reevaluate and seek out ways of using your God-given gifts more often. If you find that you are using your gifts often at the moment, that's wonderful. When and if you come to a crossroad at some point in the future and need to make decisions about a different job, relationship, or set of activities in your life, being aware of your gifts will help you focus on making choices that are consistent with these gifts.

PAYING ATTENTION TO THE WISDOM OF YOUR BODY

Another way that we listen to what our lives have to tell us is to pay attention to the clues our bodies give us. Body wisdom is a tool we often ignore in discernment. We tend to think of discernment as something we do with head and heart alone. But our bodies are gifts from God and can provide clues to God's will.

"We are to learn to listen to the signals of our bodies, honoring them as one of the main ways God speaks to us and by which we can learn much unencountered truth about ourselves and our communities,"[6] says Flora Wuellner in *Prayer and Our Bodies.* How many of us think of our bodies as one of the main ways God speaks to us? Many of us have grown accustomed to abusing or ignoring them. We eat too much or too little, or we eat too little during the day and then too much at night. We sleep too few hours, exercise less than we might, work when we are ill, and ignore all the body's signals that we are stressed. It takes a major illness to stop some of us, even when the body has been telling us for ages that it is time to stop or slow down or take better care of ourselves. All the while, we may be praying to God for guidance, but we are ignoring anything God might be saying to us through our bodies. God may be screaming to us through a variety of body ailments or through feelings of physical strength and health, but we seem to want some clearer sign—something "spiritual" rather than earthy and physical.

This is not to say that everything related to our bodies is the handiwork of God. God does not create illnesses, accidents, or other bodily events just to communicate with or punish us. To accuse a victim of cystic fibrosis, for instance, of

Lord, sanctify us wholly, that our whole spirit, soul, and body may become thy temple.

THOMAS KEN

not praying hard enough for healing, of not wanting to be well, or of being ill because of some sinfulness is cruelty beyond imagination. But our bodies do seem to know—instinctively—when we are not using our gifts, when we are making poor choices, or when we are going in a direction that is contrary to God's desires for us. Often they "hear" better and sooner than the intellect does. And they have ways of passing their information along, which we'll explore in a moment. Ordinary attentiveness to what is going on within our bodies, then, can give us clues about whether we are following or resisting God's call to us.

A friend once wrote me with a wonderful example of this. Stephen had recently left a job he had held for almost fifteen years—a job he really disliked for at least five of those fifteen years. He agonized over the decision to leave, and for many years was simply unable to decide to move on. After a lengthy vacation, he spoke to a friend about his indecision. "It wasn't until I spoke to her that I knew," he wrote me. "We were talking about my big trip, and I told her that I'd hoped to have an answer at the end of the vacation, to the question of whether or not to stay in my job, and was disappointed not to have such an answer. But as I spoke to her about it, I noticed that, when I spoke of staying in my job there was a sense of resignation, and my shoulders were slumping. But as I spoke of leaving, the world seemed full of possibilities. I was animated and excited. Somehow in the midst of

82

talking, I noticed this, and as I related this observation to my friend, I realized that my body was basically trying to tell me what it was that I wanted." Stephen's story is not a unique one; many of us can benefit from the wisdom of our bodies if we can only learn to pay attention.

Each body responds in its own way; there is no guidebook to your own physical sensations or experiences and their relationship to what is going on in your life. And it takes practice to begin noticing and using the information your body provides, especially if you are used to thinking very little about how your body feels. Generally, however, most of us know when we are feeling good and when we are feeling lousy. Stress may be accompanied by physical sensations of tightness anywhere in the body, but often in the shoulders, back, stomach, head, neck, or intestines. Short, shallow breaths may also be a symptom of stress, as is feeling cold when there isn't a particular environmental or physical reason for being chilly. When all is well with our world, however, we breathe freely, our shoulders drop away from our ears, our stomachs relax, and we are hungry at appropriate times. Under high stress or in times of great conflict, we may have trouble sleeping; at other times our sleep is deep and undisturbed. Headaches, body temperature, twitches and spasms, and a variety of other bodily reactions all have something to tell us about what is going on in the moment or in our lives in general. By knowing how your own body responds to stress, excitement, delight, fear, and other emotional states, you will have an important tool for discernment.

O Holy Spirit, love of God: Infuse your grace! O, plentifully descend into my heart. Enlighten the dark corners of this neglected building. Dwell in that soul that longs to be your temple.

SAINT AUGUSTINE

I discovered this for myself during that time when I had tried to work in the homeless shelters. Each week, before my shift began, my stomach began to tighten and get a little nauseous. My heart rate and blood pressure went up because I was feeling anxious. And I came away from each shift feeling distressed and exhausted. Others who worked at the shelter were clearly energized by the work. They came away from their shift animated and enthusiastic, the same way I felt after leading a retreat or from writing. My body was showing me where God's desires for me lay and wasn't being terribly subtle about it either.

This may be very new to you; if so, try this practice for the next seven days:

1. Make a commitment to stop and observe your body for five minutes in the morning when you get up, then around lunchtime, dinnertime, and before bed. Try to avoid being disturbed during those five-minute periods.

2. Record in a journal what you can observe about how your body is feeling at those times. Is it relaxed and warm? Or stressed and cold? (Body temperature usually rises when we are relaxed and cools when we are stressed.) Is there tightness or pain anywhere in your body? If some distress you recorded last time you did this has disappeared in the meantime, make a note of that, too. Try to record any bodily sensations you observe.

3. In the noon, evening, and nighttime sessions, think back over the hours since you last recorded what your body feels. What can you recall about

how your body responded to the events of your day or night? When did a headache or backache begin? Was it related to anything going on? When did you begin to relax? What parts of the day or events brought about feelings of excitement and energy? Which parts fatigued, depressed, or stressed you?

Each of us has a body rhythm that is natural for us. We are more alert and energized during some hours of the day and more lethargic during others. As you go through the week, take note of these patterns. Are you a morning person or a night person? Do you experience a lull at some point during each day? Knowing your body's natural responses provides clues about how to structure your day when you have a choice. I experience a lull in energy from about two to four o'clock each afternoon, for instance. That makes this a good time to do work that takes less energy from me than the work I generally do in the mornings when I am very alert. For the purposes of discernment, however, knowing the body's rhythm can help us know what times of the day are better than others for decision making.

4. Try to notice any patterns that emerge as you continue logging your experiences during the week. Are there particular things you do that increase energy and your sense of well-being? What parts of your day, work, or relationships routinely drain you? It's normal to have some parts of your life that are less engaging than others, but if that occupies a large part of your day, it is probably time to reassess your priorities and listen deeply for God's true call to you.

Once you know what your body's rhythm is, how it provides clues to what you are feeling, and whether you are involved in something that is right for you, you can use that information in everyday discerning, as well as in more complex decisions when needed. Faced with a choice to do something or move in a particular direction, you can consult your body to see if it is tightening or opening, if your breathing is shallow or full, or whatever else you know about your own body. These clues often provide early warning signs that we are on the wrong path or confirmation that we are proceeding in a way that is consistent with God's hopes for us.

HEARING THE STORY OF YOUR LIFE

Hindsight is so much clearer than foresight. I can look back on my life and find God's guidance in the various parts of my story, but looking ahead is more difficult. That's why it is important to look backward once in a while and listen to your life story. By paying attention to how your story has evolved so far, you may find important clues to discerning how to live every day, but you will also have important information to help guide you when you reach a major crossroad in your life. If, for instance, you have discovered that a growing sense of concern for God's creation—the environment around you—has been a part of your story, that informs daily decisions such as getting new plastic bags each time you shop versus bringing along a canvas bag. Knowing that God has guided you to care deeply for the Earth may also inform your next career decision, where you live, or how you raise your family.

Remember the story about Parker Palmer ignoring his depression? In *Let Your Life Speak,* he courageously tells us about ignoring his life for years and what happened:

> Imagine that from early in my life, a friendly figure, standing a block away, was trying to get my attention by shouting my name, wanting to teach me some hard but healing truths about myself. But I—fearful of what I might hear or arrogantly trying to live without help or simply too busy with my ideas and ego and ethics to bother—ignored the shouts and walked away.
>
> So this figure, still with friendly intent, came closer and shouted more loudly, but I kept walking. Even closer it came, close enough to tap me on the shoulder, but I walked on. Frustrated by my unresponsiveness, the figure threw stones at my back, then struck me with a stick, still wanting simply to get my attention. But despite the pain, I kept walking away.[7]

All this friendly figure wanted, Palmer writes, was to get him to turn around and ask, "What do you want?" That's all God wants from most of us, but it seems so much easier to turn our attention to making money, being successful, or clinging to our own sense of who we are rather than paying attention to God.

But there is great value in stopping occasionally to review the ever-changing story of our lives, to see if God is trying to tell us something. At eighteen, we tell the story one way, focusing on some thread that seems to hold it all together. When we are thirty-five, or sixty, we will tell the story very differently. In fact, the story you tell this year will probably not be the same one you tell even a year from now. A friend of mine took a three-year spiritual formation (development) program, and at the beginning of each year, members of the class were asked to write their spiritual autobiography. She was amazed that her own story changed so much from year to year. Small decisions made and small steps taken in daily life turned out, in retrospect, to have been major steps that changed the focus of her story. The same is true for all of us, so it pays us to step out of ourselves, as it were, look backward, and retell the story to ourselves or others once in a while.

That, of course, is a large assignment, but a few questions may help you break it down. In answering each of the questions that follow, try to pay attention not only to the facts and feelings of the various places and times but to your body's response—whether you are feeling anxious or excited, stressed or relaxed—and to what you are thinking and writing as well.

Before you begin, try to recall times in your life when you felt joyful or peaceful or energized or excited. These moments probably have something to do with God's call to you. You might find it helpful to record the details of these times or places. Then answer the following questions:

1. What were you doing when God called to you? Were you doing it alone or with others? What, specifically, seemed to give you joy, peace, or energy? How did you feel physically during this time? How did you come to be involved in this activity, relationship, or place? What were your greatest satisfactions or accomplishments?

2. When have you felt a sense of God's presence? Reflect on and make notes about those times. If you can, describe what God's presence felt like to you. Were the sensations physical, emotional, spiritual, or some

combination of all of these? Where were you when you felt the presence of God? What were the circumstances? How did you feel at the time?

3. When have you felt that God was guiding you? Make a list of those times. Again, can you describe what form that guidance took for you? Were there others involved, and if so how? How did you know that the guidance came from God? Was that guidance welcome or did it frighten or annoy you? What was your response to God's call for you?

4. Have there been periods of your life when anger or frustration have been regular companions? Record the details of those times. Being aware of these times and their characteristics may help you recognize times when you followed a call other than God's. How did you end up in these activities, relationships, or places? Describe the kinds of things that angered or annoyed you? How did your body fare during these periods? What was your relationship with God like during those times?

5. Are there hopes and desires—dreams—that have surfaced repeatedly in your life? What are they? Can you imagine a scenario in which they come true? What would that look like? What would be the result for

Although I have often abandoned you, O Lord, you have never abandoned me. Your hand of love is always outstretched towards me, even when I stubbornly look the other way. And your gentle voice constantly calls me, even when I obstinately refuse to listen.

TERESA OF AVILA

you and for others? Do you sense that these hopes and desires are from God, or do they arise from your ego's needs or cultural expectations? If you believe they come from God, what prevents you from acting on your heart's desires? How does your body feel as you think about these hopes?

All of these questions will help you focus on aspects of your life's story—past, present, and perhaps even future. Take as much time as you need to answer them—days, weeks, or months. By writing out your answers, you'll have something you can review. Look through what you've recorded for possible threads or patterns, highlighting words or ideas that show up repeatedly, particularly in questions 1, 2, 3, and 5. Do you notice anything that comes up over and over again? Does this give you any clue about God's call for you? Then look again at question 4. Does what you have written about what annoys and angers you tell you anything about paths you may have taken that were (or are) not part of your call? If you know which paths are wrong for you, you can more easily avoid them in the future.

God to enfold me,

God to surround me,

God in my speaking,

God in my thinking.

God in my sleeping,

God in my waking,

God in my watching,

God in my hoping.

TRADITIONAL CELTIC PRAYER

All of this, of course, is a lot of focusing on ourselves; perhaps that seems narcissistic. And if we practice an awareness of ourselves only in order to glory in how amazing we are, then the criticism would be valid. But real knowledge of God's guidance in the world begins in our own body, mind, and soul. We cannot truly know and understand how God speaks to us unless we have actually experienced it. Learning to discern the fingerprint of God on your own life allows you to know deep in your soul and your skin the person God calls you to be. Then be that person instead of trying to be what you aren't. You'll be much richer for the experience. So will the rest of the world.

Chapter Five

LEARNING WITH THE HEART

*Our pursuit of knowledge is an expression of love for God's world and
the riches of revelation. . . . Since our gifts and ministries vary we need
to encourage one another to value not only reading and study but many
other ways of learning, every method that helps us become more responsive
in heart and mind to the whole of creation.*[1]

THE RULE OF THE SOCIETY OF SAINT JOHN THE EVANGELIST

Long ago, when everything on earth
could speak and understand everything else, according to one of my favorite
children's books, *Old Turtle,*[2] an argument began. Every created thing and being insisted that God was the spitting image of itself. The wind knew God as

something always in motion, but the stones knew that God never moved. The mountains argued that God is found high above the clouds, but the fish knew better; God was found in the depths of the sea. Each thing that existed saw only one aspect of God, one consistent with their own worldview, until Old Turtle put a stop to the argument. God is all of these things, Old Turtle told them, and much more.

In Genesis, we read that we were created in the image of God, but more often than not we reverse that statement and try to create God in our own image. That's a natural tendency. We take whatever experiences we've had and whatever we've been taught, usually as children, and create a construct of God that is consistent with all of that. In discernment, this poses a difficulty, particularly when the image of God we learned from our parents is negative. Felicity Kelcourse, a professor of pastoral care and counseling, writes that we derive our God-images from our parents' behavior or ways, even when they are oppressive. "So God the Father, Mother, Creator becomes god the drunk, god the unholy terror, god the absent, unavailable father, god the poisonous mother."[3] If we limit our understanding of God to our first childhood images rather than open up our heart through study and further exploration, we put God in a tiny box. And once we've done that, discernment becomes difficult. When we hear a call that is inconsistent with our God-in-a-tiny-box, we simply dismiss it rather than use it as an opportunity to see whether it is the box or our heart that needs to be opened.

In her *Memories of God*, mentioned in Chapter Two, Roberta Bondi wrote of her struggle with coming to know a God who loved her unconditionally. Her image of God was limited and shaped by her early experiences with a faith community that spoke primarily of sinfulness and with her strict and demanding father. If her human father couldn't love her unconditionally, if she was as sinful and undeserving as she had been taught to believe, she thought, how could a heavenly Father care for her deeply? But while pursuing her academic degree at Oxford, she began reading the Desert Fathers and other early Christian writings that challenged her image of God as someone with impossibly high standards. By reading the writings and stories of those who knew a loving God, Bondi was exposed to views and experiences that differed radically from her own. She could have closed her heart to those views. Instead, she allowed her studies to help her clarify what she had learned in childhood and then to open her heart to the possibility that her views might be limited. That, in turn, gave her the confidence to seek the God she read about—the loving God these early Christians knew. Once she began to know a loving God, she was able to discern that God called her to stop living as a second-class person.

Old Turtle and Roberta Bondi's stories highlight a common bias in practicing discernment. We tend to rely almost exclusively on, and get trapped by, our feelings and our own experiences when discerning God's guidance in our lives. Each of the things and beings in *Old Turtle* automatically assumes that God is just like itself. Roberta Bondi accepted her childhood feelings about God as fact, but her studies contradicted them. Although paying attention to our feelings is absolutely essential to the process (we would be unable to discern God's will without them), we also need to pay attention to our minds and intellects. Study, as a spiritual discipline, provides an important counterbalance for our feelings. Recall that the ancient Hebrews saw the heart as the center of intellect, as well as emotion and spiritual life. "At the heart of the spiritual life is the attention to the cognitive process," writes Urban Holmes, an Episcopal priest, in his book *Spirituality for Ministry*.[4] "What is it we know?" The hearing heart needs to know what it knows. It needs the nourishment of study as much as it needs prayer and traditional spiritual practices. Study develops an informed heart and deepens the heart's ability to hear clearly. Scripture is the basis of that study, but reading books other than the Bible, looking at or creating art, listening to or playing music, acting, as well as a variety of other types of study or observation, can also help you develop a heart that is truly open to God's guidance.

SEEING WITH OUR LENSES

Like Roberta Bondi, each of us has a lens through which we look at and evaluate the world around us. It's both unavoidable and healthy to have a lens that helps us make sense of everything we see and experience. We create ways of categorizing information, as well as the things that happen to us that are based in the values of the places we have lived, the institutions we've been affiliated with, our schooling, the values and understandings of friends and family, and our own experiences. All of that is well and good. But when we are unconscious of that lens— when we think that the way we see and understand is Reality—we limit our ability to discern well. We will end up forcing God into our systems of thinking rather than expanding the mind of our heart to accommodate God.

Leo Tolstoy, the great Russian writer, told a story once of three hermits who challenged the lens of a bishop. While the bishop was sailing to a monastery, three ostensibly holy hermits who lived on an obscure island in the middle of the sea came to his attention. Wanting to meet these holy men, the bishop landed on the island and began asking the men about their spiritual practices and understandings. Finding their answers deficient, he taught them the basics of his theology and instructed them in saying the Lord's Prayer. Much satisfied with his efforts, he returned to the ship. Later that evening, as the ship sailed on, he saw the hermits running rapidly across the water, desperate to reach the bishop. They had forgotten how to say the Lord's Prayer and wished to be taught the prayer again. "Your own prayer will reach the Lord, men of God. It is not for me to teach you. Pray for us sinners," responded the bishop, who now understood his own arrogance versus the humility of the three holy men.[5] The bishop's narrow lens—one that encouraged exact knowledge of his understanding of theology and specific prayer practices in order to know God—was shattered by the lives of the three holy men who worshiped and served God in a different way. Instead of seeing himself as the wise teacher, he was forced to understand that he was their pupil instead.

> *O Lord, heavenly Father, in whom is the fullness of light and wisdom, enlighten our minds by your Holy Spirit, and give us grace to receive your Word with reverence and humility, without which no one can understand your truth.*
>
> JOHN CALVIN

Most of us don't get to experience the three holy hermits regularly, however, and study helps us understand and clarify the lens through which we look. By studying, I don't just mean reading a snippet of the Bible each day. "[A] vast difference exists between the study of Scripture and the devotional reading of

Scripture," writes Quaker author Richard Foster. "In the study of Scripture a high priority is placed upon interpretation: what it means. In the devotional reading of Scripture a high priority is placed upon application: what it means for me."[6]

Both ways of reading are important in opening the heart, and we'll look at each of them in this chapter. But frequently we are more interested in personal meaning than the context of the story or its meaning to the writer or the first communities who heard the stories. In order to know the lens through which we look, it is important to study critically, to ask if what we are reading or observing is consistent with what we already believe, if it challenges what we believe, and if our beliefs need to be amended.

When we read scripture, for instance, we tend to gloss over the inconsistencies in the way the gospel stories are told. We might skip reading sections of the Bible that we find offensive or too violent. All of that might be reasonable, but we need to know why we are eliminating or ignoring a given passage or story. The same is true with all reading and studying. If we cannot be clear with ourselves about what we believe—very specifically—we will be confused about our sense of God's guidance as well. If we cannot read the stories of how God guided our ancestors with a discerning head and heart, how will we look at our own stories that way?

Your word is a lamp to my feet and a light to my path.

PSALM 119:105

As a young child, I came face-to-face with two possible lenses through which to see God. The conflict between the two lenses (most of which was unconscious until I began to explore it) resulted in tremendous feelings of frustration, even despair at times. Somewhere in the deepest recesses of my memory lives my first glimmer of God's invitation to me, of God's desire for me. I have always associated the memory with the Unitarian congregation that we belonged to when I was quite young—less than two years old. I remember the whole congregation sitting in a circle that fills the room. Parents are holding some of their squirming children lovingly while other children play on the floor, and a sense of community fills the scene. The room is drenched in bright gold-colored light that seems to enter the room from every possible angle. That light, which is for me the presence of God, bathes me in warmth. I am aware of feeling comforted, held, and secure at the deepest possible level. I am vibrant and alive but also quiet and centered. I am one not only with God but with everyone in the room, with the room itself. I know that I am

Take away, O Lord, the veil of my heart while I read the scriptures. Blessed art thou, O Lord: O teach me thy statutes! Give me a word, O Word of the Father; touch my heart: enlighten the understandings of my heart: open my lips and fill them with thy praise.

LANCELOT ANDREWES

loved deeply and unconditionally. I have no idea if all of this is an actual memory, a dream, or a vision of some sort, but it is my first conscious experience of God's presence.

When I began to attend church school, another image of God became dominant, and I started to look through this new lens most of the time. My earliest memory of a picture of God from those years gets confused with pictures of Moses holding the Ten Commandments. God was male; the idea of a feminine God was not even thought of at that time. God was an old man with a white beard, wearing white robes, holding up a tablet with the Ten Commandments on it for all to see and follow. God was about power and rules. Whereas my early vision of God left me with the knowledge that we are all one, my church school training taught me about "us and them." There were Christians, and then there was everyone else. There were good girls and boys, and bad ones. It was always clear that being one of "us" was better.

The vision of a comforting God who brings light and healing and love was all but gone through most of my childhood. That God was not entirely absent, but his (God was a "he" during that time) presence was muted. Instead, God was someone with whom we made deals: if we were good, we would be rewarded; if we were bad, we would be punished. God was the God in a song my dad used to sing to us at bedtime. A preacher went hunting one Sunday morning. Not only is he where he is not supposed to be on a Sunday morning but the song says that hunting is against his religion. And he sins even further by shooting some quail and a rabbit. As he is headed home, he encounters a grizzly bear that corners the preacher, high up in a persimmon tree. It is time to try to make a deal with God, so the preacher begs that if God can't help him, God should at least refrain from helping the bear.

In the end, the song leaves the preacher's fate a little ambiguous. The bear shakes the preacher out of the tree and hugs him "just a little too tight." When we are bad, the song implies, there are no deals with God; the deal hinges on our being good, or at the very least, on being very sorry for what we have done wrong.

All of this affected my ability to discern who and what I was called to be for many years. Because my sense of being God's beloved had been replaced by a sense of God as one who judged me harshly—a God I feared—I did not seek or have any sense of God's will. It was better to stay beneath God's radar if at all possible. I found myself working in positions that didn't use my gifts, and when I did poorly in the job, I was prone to believe that I was being "bad" somehow, that I lacked much in the way of skills. But in my late twenties, I began taking classes that explored the Bible and spiritual disciplines. I began reading the Bible and other religious books and talked with others about their understandings. It was in the midst of this intentional study time that I realized the truth of my earliest vision of God. I put God the judge and deal maker behind me and began listening more intently and intentionally to the God who loves me and calls me forth into the world.

Oddly enough, that very early vision of God was a clue to one of my own gifts, which is the ability to see what an organization can become. Perhaps, even from my youngest days, God was trying to show me that I had the gift of vision. Much of my professional career has been based on trusting the vision I am given of an organization's potential. If I had retained my sense of God as the deal maker and judge, I would have been afraid to follow my gut feelings about upend-

> *I am the LORD your God, who teaches you for your own good, who leads you in the way you should go.*
>
> PSALM 48:17

ing the way things had always been in places where I've worked. I would have been the "good girl" who followed the rules. Taking classes, reading, studying, talking with others, listening to sermons, and letting myself be challenged by other viewpoints has helped me clarify which lens produces a clearer, truer image of God's will for my own life.

In the past few decades, many groups of people have begun defining how their image of God affects their ability to discern and act on who they are called

Then Jesus said to the Jews who had believed in him, "If you continue in my word, you are truly my disciples; and you will know the truth, and the truth will make you free."

JOHN 8:31–32

to be. Feminists began reading the Bible through their own eyes and have shared how they see God. People of color have written and spoken about the lens through which they view God. Gays and lesbians, people with disabilities, singles, and others are also sharing their stories today. Each of these perspectives invites us to look at what we think we know and discover anew that God will always be bigger and more than any one of us knows.

Studying opens the doorway into your heart. It provides you with glimpses of God's truth, of God's desires. Far too often, however, we think study provides us with final and complete answers. Our early schooling conditioned us to think that way, especially in its use of tests with right answers. But studying for the purposes of discernment helps us open our minds, souls, and hearts to all of the ways in which God operates and communicates. It doesn't give us exact scientific answers; in fact, sometimes it leaves us with more questions than we had before we began looking at a new perspective.

But the desire to find final answers and extract them from what we choose to study needs to be resisted if we are to discern well. Catholic priest and author Anthony De Mello tells the story of a man who had been declared dead and was then buried alive. The man began pounding on the coffin lid and demanding to be let out. "Friend, both the doctors and the priests have certified that you are dead. So dead you are," said his friends. And so he was buried.[7] Far too often, we use scripture and other study in this way—as final, irrefutable answers to our questions or concerns, even when we know that our knowledge of scripture is sometimes quite limited and that scripture is full of contradictory information and images. When we search the scriptures in order to justify a point of view we already hold or want to hold, we are engaging in a process called proof-texting. We can find and justify any answer we are seeking if we look hard enough. But the purpose of studying is to discern more clearly. What we read, analyze, view, or otherwise observe provides us with the opportunity to know our own lens and to challenge it by learning about the lenses of others. —— *Open Lens, "Unwritten" Lens.*

GETTING STARTED

If you haven't done much in-depth study of scripture, let me suggest some ways of getting started.

❀ *Choose an entire book of the Bible to read all the way through.* Most of us have heard bits and pieces from many books of the Bible but have not read entire books. Genesis, Exodus, and Numbers, in the Old Testament, and the gospels of Matthew, Mark, or Luke make good starting places, if you haven't read them. You could choose to read the book over a weekend or take a longer period of time—a week or month—to read. You might also include these systematic readings in your own daily prayer times. You might find it very helpful to use a Bible that has study aids in it. A basic Bible commentary is another good companion for your reading because it provides historical context, interpretation of difficult phrases or concepts, and other information.

❀ *Choose a shorter book of the Bible.* In his book *Celebration of Discipline*, Richard Foster suggests choosing a shorter book, such as one of the Epistles (the letters in the New Testament), and reading it through completely each day for a month. Again, a Bible with study aids and the use of a commentary can help you gain a critical understanding of what you read.[8]

❀ *Try to discover what the author of a particular book is trying to say.* Whatever you read, try to see what the author's image of God is. How did that image affect the way the author told the story? Do these stories affect your own image of God and God's ways of acting in the world? If they do, how do your ideas differ from what the writer of the biblical text is trying to say? What do you need to do about any views that are contrary to your own?

❀ *Take courses.* Another approach to study that can be helpful, particularly if you are new to reading the Bible or other religious books, is to take one or more religion or spirituality courses. Whether from your local university, college, seminary, or in classes offered within parish settings, study of this kind, along with others, may provide you with helpful information, historical context, or other perspectives that open the doors to studying as a way of listening for God's will and guidance in your own life.

"Study is not done for mere curiosity for learning but because wisely ordered reading endows the mind with greater steadiness and serves as a basis for the contemplation of God in [the] world,"[9] says a contemporary monastic guidebook. And that is the reason we read and study widely. It provides us with a solid basis for understanding God's guidance in the world and, with that in hand, for God's guidance in our own lives.

SACRED READING TO OPEN THE HEART

Devotional reading is one of the ways of opening the mind of our heart to God's will and guidance, particularly as it relates to our own lives. But devotional reading doesn't mean that we turn off the mind of our heart. We don't treat this kind of reading or studying as a kind of tarot reading, opening the Bible at random, with the assumption that God will guide us to exactly the right page and passage that answers our question. Lectio divina, a Latin term for sacred reading, a practice inherited from early monastic literature and life, points us clearly toward a deep understanding of sacred texts that can change what we understand and how we live. "Lectio includes reading, private prayer, and meditatio," writes Kevin Irwin, in the *New Dictionary of Catholic Spirituality,* "with 'meditation' meaning the memorization and prayerful rumination . . . of texts as a stimulus to personal prayer. The desired result of application to lectio divina is a thorough assimilation of sacred truth and *a life lived according to this truth"* (emphasis mine).[10]

Martin Luther, who once taught scripture studies at the University of Wittenberg, approached devotional reading in much the same spirit. He read small portions of biblical texts in a prayerful way but with the assumption that he would find within it instruction, reasons for offering thanksgiving to God, things he needed to confess, and guidance for his life. His was a devotional approach but, as professor of spirituality Joseph Driskill explains in his exploration of Luther's approach, Luther believed that "the one praying begins with an awareness that the text offers instruction that may be informed by scholarly study."[11] In other words, you read scripture, or even other texts, in a meditative way but not one divorced from critical or scholarly study. You can ponder them deeply in order to discern God's truth and to live according to that truth.

For example, take the text from Luke 1 containing the angel's announcement to Mary about the impending birth of Jesus:

> The angel said to her, "The Holy Spirit will come upon you, and the power of the Most High will overshadow you; therefore the child to be born will be holy; he will be called Son of God. And now, your relative Elizabeth in her old age has also conceived a son; and this is the sixth month for her who was said to be barren. For nothing will be impossible with God." Then Mary said, "Here am I, the servant of the Lord; let it be with me according to your word." Then the angel departed from her. (Luke 1:35–38)

We read this passage during Advent each year, and inevitably preachers praise Mary for her obedience. If we read uncritically, the lesson for a person trying to discern and live God's will appears to be that, once you know God's desires, you should agree to them with no thought or hesitation. Mary has the time it takes for the angel to get out the sentence about Elizabeth for her response—maybe a couple of seconds. I don't know about you, but I find the idea of being given only an instant to respond to God's call pretty frightening. If all we knew about the call to Mary was this passage from Luke, we might give up even trying to discern God's will for fear that we'd be given only seconds to act on it.

But by studying the biblical texts more widely, you'll discover that Matthew is the only other gospel to even hint at this story. Matthew says that Mary was found to be with child from the Holy Spirit (Matthew 1:18). He doesn't tell us that she had just a second to make a decision. Mark and John don't mention anything about the annunciation to Mary. So maybe we don't have just a few seconds after all to respond to God's call. Acting on God's desires—obedience—is important, but maybe we get to think about our response.

Over the past few years, I have come across two other interpretations of the Annunciation that open up these texts in meaningful ways for me, both of them works of art. The first is a painting titled "The Annunciation," painted by Henry Ossawa Tanner. (This painting is easy to locate on the Internet.) Mary sits on the bed of her room and a bright pillar of light, the angel, stands at the opposite end of the room. Mary has a distrustful, dubious expression on her face, as if she were questioning the reality of what the angel is saying. Her look is almost defiant. She seems to want proof that this is a call from God and that she has to accept it.

*Almighty God, our heavenly Father, without whose help labour is useless,
without whose light search is vain, invigorate my studies and direct my enquiries,
that I may by due diligence and right discernment establish myself . . . in thy
holy Faith. . . . Let me not linger in ignorance and doubt, but enlighten
and support me for the sake of Jesus Christ our Lord. Amen.*

SAMUEL JOHNSON

The second is in a children's book, *The Nativity*, illustrated by Julie Vivas.[12] The wonderfully fanciful artwork features Angel Gabriel and Mary discussing this announcement over a cup of tea or coffee at the kitchen table. Their elbows are on the table, and they are leaning in toward each other. Gabriel appears to be listening intently and patiently to Mary, who looks a bit surprised.

Hear this, all you peoples; give ear,
all inhabitants of the world, both low
and high, rich and poor together.
My mouth shall speak wisdom;
the meditation of my heart shall
be understanding.

PSALM 49:1–3

Bringing both of these images to a critical reading of the text from Luke, I understand the passage and its implications for God's guidance in my own life differently than I would if I just read Luke without engaging my heart and mind. Mary's obedience to God's call is still primary, and it invites me to accept God's call when I hear it in my own life. But the interpretation of the two painters suggests that I am allowed to be skeptical or intimidated or just plain surprised about what I hear about God's desires for me. I get to discuss them and ask questions. God's call isn't going to be like a game show where I have a limited time to give the right response. All of this illustrates a way we can use devotional reading to open our hearts and prepare them to discern God's will. Although the biblical texts are foundational for us, we often breeze through them, particularly the stories we know well, and barely notice the details of the story or stop to think about them. Reading and studying paintings, drama, music, and even nature can help open us up to the biblical stories in new ways and hear them at a much deeper level.

Martin Luther's way of reading and praying scripture is another way of exploring the texts devotionally. As mentioned earlier, he focused his praying and reading on what he called a four-stranded garland. Each reading focused on one of four strands, which were united at the end to form a "garland." Try this exercise with the passage we've been exploring in Luke. (I am indebted to Joe Driskill for this practice, which can be found in *Protestant Spiritual Exercises;* see especially pages 92–97.)

1. Read the passage through four times, either silently or aloud. Try to read the passage slowly, without rushing. If a word or phrase jumps out at you, you might even choose to repeat it or pause to savor it for a moment. Each time you read, focus on one of the four suggestions that follow. You may find it helpful to respond to the questions by recording words or thoughts that come to mind.

2. Ask yourself, in this first reading, what instruction you find in the passage. Is there a word or a phrase that seems to speak to you in this time and place? Make some notes to yourself about what you hear of instruction in the reading if you want to.

3. Read the passage a second time. Remember to read slowly so you can pay close attention to it. This time, ask yourself if there is something you've read that brings about a sense of gratitude in you. Again, make some notes about this if you find that helpful.

4. Read the passage a third time. See if there is something that challenges the way you are living or that brings about a need to confess or for

which you need to apologize to God. Do you find something that suggests that you are not currently listening to God with your heart or following God's will for your life?

5. Read the passage a final time. During this final reading, rest in the knowledge that God is, indeed, guiding you in these words, even if you do not know how this is happening. You may want to end your reading and reflection time with a prayer.

This method of reading is a combination of reading and studying, along with reflection or meditation, but its focus is on listening very intentionally for God's guidance. Remember that what you are reading probably speaks to you in the context of today and does not need to be an answer—and certainly not *the* answer—for your life as a whole. But using this exercise with some regularity will help you learn to read or study with the desire of seeking God's will rather than just for knowledge alone or for entertainment.

This kind of reading is often practiced with the Bible or with classic spiritual literature such as the Desert Fathers, or books about the lives of the saints. But it can be beneficial to read other books this way as well. As odd as it may sound, I find a great deal of illumination and guidance in my collection of mysteries with religious characters and themes. One of my favorite mysteries, for instance, deals with the question of redemption and how we find God's (and our own) forgiveness for acts we consider unforgivable. Others explore the role of discernment in unraveling the mystery or the place of retreat in the spiritual life. All of them provide a relaxing and sometimes challenging way to explore spiritual and theological issues.

But you don't need to limit yourselves to studying only through reading. As the quote at the beginning of the chapter reminds us, "Since our gifts and ministries vary we need to encourage one another to value not only reading and study but many other ways of learning, every method that helps us become more responsive in heart and mind to the whole of creation." For many people, art, music, and drama are important ways of studying.

Religious art is an obvious example. We have many centuries worth of paintings, sculptures, stained-glass windows, and other artistic interpretations of biblical texts and messages, many of them designed specifically to teach. Before books and literacy became more common, stained-glass windows in churches and cathedrals retold the stories of the Bible so that people could learn them. You can still look at the windows and ask yourself if the artist's interpretation of the story and of God's movement in the world matches yours or if they have something to teach you at this time.

Grant me, I beseech you, O merciful God, prudently to study, rightly to understand and perfectly to fulfill that which is pleasing to you, to the praise and glory of your name. Amen.

ADAPTED FROM THOMAS AQUINAS

Another fascinating example of the power of art to teach is the proliferation in the last few years of icons, especially icons from perspectives different from the traditional Western, Christian ones. An icon is a painting of a saint, usually from a two-dimensional perspective—a technique developed by Orthodox Christians;

the use of icons has spread to people of various faiths in recent years. What does an image of a black Christ have to teach you or an icon of Christ Sophia—a feminine image of Christ? How do these expand the lens through which you see God or receive guidance?

The same is true of classic and contemporary drama, poetry, and music based on religious themes. The stories are told, and we can be in dialogue with them, first through the artist's or writer's eyes and then within the mind of our own hearts, just as I was with the Tanner painting of the Annunciation. All of these can be avenues for clarifying the lens through which we look at God and for opening the mind of the heart to God's word and God's guidance in our lives. After all, God's ability to speak to us can take many different forms. Why limit ourselves to listening to God only in one way?

Chapter Six

DISCERNING COMPANIONS

Thus God announces that He does not want the soul to believe only by itself the communications it thinks are of divine origin, or anyone to be assured or confirmed in them without the Church or her ministers. God will not bring clarification and confirmation of the truth to the heart of one who is alone. Such a person would remain weak and cold in regard to truth.

JOHN OF THE CROSS, *THE ASCENT OF MOUNT CARMEL*

In one of my favorite murder mysteries, the lead character, Brother Bartholomew, struggles with what feels to him like a call away from the monastery. Deeply conflicted, he asks his spiritual adviser for help. "What do you think God wants you to do?" Brother Anselm asks. "What's coming to me," says Bartholomew, "is that He may want me to become involved, but not *involved.*" Brother Anselm questions Bartholomew for a while and asks him to think about what he truly wants, deep in his heart. Bartholomew realizes that though he feels called to help the chief of police, a friend of his, with solving crimes occasionally, his true call is to the monastic life. "Then that is precisely why God can trust you to help your friend without fear of losing your spiritual center,"[1] Anselm reminds Bartholomew.

Bartholomew tied himself up in knots trying to discern what God had called him to do. But Anselm saw clearly what Bartholomew could not see for himself—that there was no conflict between Bartholomew's call to the monastic life and his occasional adventure helping his police chief friend solve mysteries. Anselm is just the kind of person we want to consult when we are trying to discern God's will. He asks questions and makes observations; he does not pretend that he knows what God is calling us to do.

Sometimes—perhaps often—in the midst of trying to sort out God's will from everything else, others can read our heart's desires and God's call to us more clearly than we can. Maybe you've had the same experience I've had of trying to make a decision, only to find that you can talk yourself into going in one direction as easily as another. I'm reminded of a television commercial in which one cube of cheese remains on the tray, and three guys are trying to decide if they should break the rules they learned as children and take the sole remaining piece. The first man has an angel on his shoulder, and on the second man's shoulder sits his mother. Both figures remind the men that it is rude to eat the last morsel of food on the tray. The third

For where two or three are gathered in my name, I am there among them.

MATTHEW 18:20

Hearing with the Heart

man has a devil on his shoulder who advises him to forget the rules and eat the cheese, which he does. When trying to make a decision, it often feels as though there's an angel on one shoulder, pointing us along one path, and a devil on the other, with an equally convincing argument. If we had just an "angel" or just a "devil" to listen to, we'd have no problem making a decision. But usually we have a little of each, and we find ourselves torn between the voices. We become like a hamster on a wheel going round and round, getting absolutely nowhere.

So far in this book, we've explored the kinds of skills we need to discern God's will. But accurate discernment calls for a balance between listening for God's call to you in the quiet spaces of your own heart and paying attention to the observations and questions of others. If you want to avoid ending up like the hamster on a wheel, you'll need help from others in the discernment process.

I was doing the hamster-on-a-wheel routine recently. I'd written something that I wasn't sure I should try to publish. It was quite different from the rest of what I had written, and I wasn't sure of its worth. After staring at it for many months, unable to make a decision, I sent it to a friend whose opinion I value. She read it thoughtfully and told me that it was well worth pursuing publication, and she told me why she thought that was so. She also told me that a few parts of it were off-target (actually, *silly* was her word, bless her heart!), and her reasons for saying so were quite convincing. I could have stared at that project for many more months and probably come to no conclusion about it, but my friend, seeing from a fresh perspective, readily saw the project for what it was.

We also need spiritual community—be that one person or a group—to help us stay focused on God rather than our own ego needs. The hermits who went out into the Egyptian and Syrian deserts in the third and fourth centuries came face-to-face with the difficulties of discerning God's will outside of community. The actions of those like our poor monk, Hero, and the young man who died in the desert instead of eating food the barbarians brought him, led Desert Fathers such as Pachomius and Basil to establish monasteries. They had discovered that those who tried to be their own spiritual guides in the desert often ended up hurting themselves—body, mind, and soul—instead of growing closer to God. The monasteries provided an alternative way of seeking God by being places where everyone in the community received guidance and help, where all had access to the wisdom of those who had walked further down the spiritual path. In the monastery, if you discerned that God wanted you to jump down a deep well, you had to check in with someone else before taking action.

That doesn't mean you have to head for the monastery every time you need advice or guidance. But we would do well to heed the voices from these communities who counsel us and listen to the sage advice of those who have walked the path before us. "We will most easily come to a precise knowledge of true discernment," wrote John Cassian, "if we follow the paths of our elders . . . and if we do not presume to decide anything on the basis of our own judgment."[2] That advice might sound a bit stodgy and old-fashioned today, and Cassian was the first to admit that some elders were far from wise. But his basic premise is that if you think you have a situation that no one else has ever seen before, and there is no one with knowledge or insight to illuminate our path, you are probably misguided.

In fact, one of the danger signs for us comes when we feel that we can't share what we are discerning with anyone else—that no one will understand our decision. When we feel that we must keep what we are doing a secret from everyone else, we are usually following a voice other than God's. That doesn't mean that you shouldn't be judicious about sharing your heart's desires and your sense of God's guidance with other people, but when a demand for total secrecy exists, either within yourself or given to you by someone else, something is usually wrong. Sometimes we give the order for secrecy to ourselves, knowing that we are not following God's will, and we want to shield ourselves from the eyes of others, even from God. When someone else tells us that we must remain silent—about a relationship or anything else—they are usually trying to prevent others from finding out that they feel they are doing something wrong. If we cannot discuss what we are discerning with others and receive confirmation or encouragement along the path we are pursuing, we will remain, as John Cassian says, "weak and cold in regard to the truth."

We need to surround ourselves with those who can help us discern and stay on the path, but we also need spiritual companions who can encourage us and, sometimes, be our champions. The process of learning to listen to God and follow God's call is never an easy one, and we need others who can help us stay focused, who can encourage us when the going gets tough.

John Cassian tells the story of a young monk who is deeply troubled by his inability to master his physical desires. Hoping that others could guide him, he sought out an older and "exemplary" monk and asked the man to pray for and help him. Instead of a sympathetic response, the old monk chastised the young one and told him he was unworthy to be a monk at all. The young monk went away in utter misery and despair. Walking along the road, he encountered Apollo, the holiest of all the monks. Apollo sensed that something was wrong and finally prevailed upon the young monk to tell his story. Apollo sympathized with the young man and told him that, even now, he still struggled with the desires of the flesh and that this was normal. He counseled the young monk not to give up, so the young monk went back to his cell (room) and continued to live the monastic life.

These kinds of spiritual friends are invaluable when we are trying to discern and live out God's desires for us. Obstacles to hearing and following our heart and paying attention to God's will cross our paths constantly. Loving companions can help us notice them, name them, and move ahead on the path to God.

SOUL FRIENDS

Sometimes confirmation or clarification of God's desires for us comes from casual acquaintances or even complete strangers. We're considering a new career direction, and someone compliments us on being skilled in just the area we are thinking about. We can't discount these occurrences as meaningless; God can speak to us through a perfect stranger as readily as through dear friends. But our soul friends are often the most helpful when we are trying to discern our way on the path.

Cassian called these spiritual advisers elders, but the Celts in Ireland and in the British Isles called them soul friends, which better describes their role in our lives today. Soul friends are those special people who care about our spiritual journey, who can walk alongside us as teacher, companion, or spiritual ʒ With a soul friend, "you are understood as you are without mask or preten: says John O'Donohue, Catholic priest and writer. "When you are unders you are at home. Understanding nourishes belonging. When you really feel understood, you feel free to release your self into the trust and shelter of the other person's soul."[3]

Anselm, the monk from the story at the start of this chapter, was Bartholomew's elder and soul friend. Bartholomew always sought Anselm to advise him when he was troubled. No matter what Anselm was doing, he stopped and listened to Bartholomew, asked questions, and made observations. Bartholomew knew that Anselm understood him and would not judge him. But he could also count on Anselm to ask good, probing questions that opened up new perspectives for Bartholomew. He knew that Anselm would speak the truth as he saw it, even when that truth might be difficult for Bartholomew to hear.

For I am longing to see you so that I may share with you some spiritual gift to strengthen you—or rather so that we may be mutually encouraged by each other's faith, both yours and mine.

ROMANS 1:11–12

That is what makes soul friends so valuable in discernment. We are all surrounded by plenty of people who feel free to give us advice on a moment's notice, even when they've just met us. Sometimes that advice is even sound or insightful. But soul friends are those who listen more deeply for God's call to us, who are comfortable waiting for God's wisdom to be revealed rather than jumping in with their own opinion. They know our faults and difficulties—what "games" we tend to play in our own hearts and minds. But they understand us and care for us in a profound way, so much so that we are willing to trust them with our soul's concerns and desires. They are also people who see with the eyes and ears of the heart, with compassion, concern, and clarity. They are the ones who, when we think our only choices are to go forward or backward on the wheel, can help us discover that perhaps God is calling us to step off the wheel and go in a whole new direction.

CHOOSING SOUL FRIENDS

The number of soul friends in most people's lives is usually small, even for those who have lots of other kinds of friends. I think of those who have listened to my struggles and my desires over the years. There is the man, a decade or so older than me, whom I see only occasionally now that we live on opposite sides of the country. He always listens to me so intently and isn't afraid to ask me really tough questions. There are also a couple of female friends who listen to what I'm saying, who hear between the lines. They are good at asking questions, at not judging, and they resist the common impulse we all have to offer lots of advice. And I can't forget the woman who began as a professional mentor, who saw who I was all the way at the core and put opportunity after opportunity in front of me until I, too, knew what she was seeing. She's long since become a trusted friend who continues to help me pay attention to God's deepest desires for me.

There have been a handful of others in my life as well. All of them share some traits in common with others who make good soul friends: they are the kind of people who can be trusted to be present, attentive, and patient when you are trying to discern God's call in your life. And here are more ways to distinguish soul friends:

🟊 *Soul friends know how to listen.* How many times have you started telling someone about something in your life only to have them chime in with a response that begins with "I had the same experience last summer when. . . ." or some other response that turns the conversation away from what you were saying? We're all guilty of this at times, but good listeners do it less often than the rest of us. Good listeners avoid formulating their next comment while we're still speaking—a practice that prevents us from really hearing what is being said by someone else. They're not afraid of silence in the conversation while they think about what you've said and about what response to make. If soul friends are to help you discover God's desires, they must be willing to listen for God as the third party in the conversation.

> *O God almighty, by whom and before whom we are all brethren: grant us so truly to love one another, that evidently and beyond all doubt we may love thee; through Jesus Christ thy Son, our Lord and brother.*
>
> CHRISTINA ROSSETTI

🟊 *Soul friends ask questions rather than give advice.* They don't jump to conclusions and offer advice. I remember a retreat I attended once, where early in the day one of the participants spoke of some troubles in her life. A couple of the other participants jumped right into the conversation and gave her the answers for her dilemma. Having known her for a couple of hours, they felt they knew exactly what she should do. It's a natural human tendency to want to fix others. We do it partly out of a desire to be helpful. But we also do it because we want to avoid really listening to or feeling someone else's pain or emotional distress; we want to make uncomfortable feelings go away. Good listeners know how to be present to what you're saying without jumping in with advice on how they handled things when faced with the same circumstances. A good listener knows that no two people are alike and that two people in the same circumstance won't have the same experience or necessarily find the same solution helpful. They ask questions—sometimes hard and clarifying ones—that help us see God's will more clearly for ourselves.

❋ *Soul friends don't judge, but they're not afraid to ask hard questions either.* They are people who listen to us with an open heart, who ask questions without a specific agenda behind them and without needing to get specific answers from us. And they avoid being judgmental about our choices. But if they are honest and care deeply about us, they won't be afraid of asking questions that might be painful or difficult to answer. They don't ask them to cause us discomfort, but they will take a risk when they think it might be important to do so. Many years ago, during a rather bleak time in my life, one of my dearest friends listened to my distress for several months. One day she very gently asked me if I had considered medication to help me through my depression. I wish I could tell you that I was grateful for the question at the time, but, in truth, it made me angry. I felt as if she was telling me that I couldn't manage my life without help; in fact, that was exactly what she was suggesting. It took a few weeks to heal the rift that

Your love, Jesus, is an ocean with no shore to bound it. And if I plunge into it, I carry with me all the possessions I have. You know, Lord, what these possessions are— the souls you have seen fit to link with mine.

THÉRÈSE OF LISIEUX

question created between us, but we muddled our way through finally. Her question, however, was a wake-up call for me; I began to realize just how depressed I really was and to face that and work toward a solution. I realized that her question was asked out of kindness and concern rather than as a judgment on me. She believed that God desired a more joyful life for me, and she was willing to call that to my attention. I came to know that she had risked a great deal and that she was truly a valued soul friend.

⁕ *Soul friends are good observers.* They often spot patterns or progressions in our lives that we're unable to notice. This is particularly helpful when we're in the midst of discerning a new direction for our lives. More often than not, we are so close to our own lives that we lack perspective on what's developing. A good soul friend is a bit like a detective who stands back and observes, looking intently for clues that bring the whole truth into perspective.

⁕ *Soul friends admit that they don't have all the answers.* Anthony De Mello, a Catholic priest and storyteller, told a simple story about a master and a disciple. The disciple complained to the master that the master told stories regularly but never explained them to the disciple. The master responded very simply: "How would you like it if someone offered you fruit and masticated it before giving it to you?"[4] Soul friends listen, they reflect on what they hear, they ask questions that help us become clearer, but they can't tell us what the right answer is. We can listen to our soul friends and take any questions they ask or comments they've made into account, but a good soul friend is not offended when we decide that we have to chew on the "fruit" and digest it for ourselves. They might point us along a particular path. They might even fervently pray that we take that path. But they won't block us from choosing another path if we discern that it is more in accordance with God's desires. And they won't say, "I told you so," if we discover that we took the wrong path after all.

So who are the soul friends who might bring some wisdom to bear on your discernment? Some of us naturally find soul friends in the course of our lives. But if you haven't consulted people as soul friends before or if no names come to mind immediately, try the following:

1. Write down the characteristics of a soul friend, leaving space between each entry.

2. Under each characteristic (for example, "good listener," "asks good questions"), write down the names of the people you already know who demonstrate that skill.

3. Take note of any names that come up repeatedly. Is it possible that one or more of these people would make a good soul friend for you?

4. Spend the next few days or longer, if needed, to hold the names of potential soul friends before God in your prayer time. Finding the right soul friend or friends is as much a matter for discernment as other important decisions in your life. Pay attention to any sense of peacefulness, correctness, or excitement that you feel. This usually indicates that you have made a good choice. Pay attention, too, to any feelings or senses of anxiety, dread, or concern. Unless you are highly self-deceptive, these are probably warnings that you have selected the wrong person.

5. When you sense that you have the right person in mind as a soul friend, approach that person and ask if he or she would be willing to listen to you and help you discern the right path. There is no right or wrong way to do this, and there is no way to avoid feeling vulnerable to a possible rejection. It is helpful, however, to ask the person about his or her willingness to help you rather than simply launch into your concern in the hope that this is the right person at this given moment. Your request conveys respect for your friend's time and energies. It also allows your friend to respond knowledgably and fully rather than have to guess about what is being asked.

6. If your friend is willing, set aside some time to explore the concern or dilemma with him or her. You'll know pretty quickly if this person is a good companion on the path for you. If the person listens, asks questions, and is attentive to what you (and God) may be saying between the lines, you've found a good soul friend. If your friend starts talking about himself or herself right away or offering advice, you may need to make another choice.

Sometimes we just need to consult about our discernment with a soul friend occasionally. A conversation here and there is all the help we need. At other times, particularly when we are trying to make decisions with serious or long-term consequences, we may need someone who can listen to us over a period of time. If you find yourself in the

> *Let the LORD your God show us where we should go and what we should do.*
>
> JEREMIAH 42:3

latter category, you might find it helpful to make an agreement with your soul friend to meet regularly (weekly, bi-weekly, or monthly) until you feel you know what God is calling you to do.

WISE GUIDANCE: THE SPIRITUAL DIRECTOR

In my own life, I've found that having a wise spiritual director is supremely helpful when I am trying to discern God's desires for me, both in the everyday things and in those moments when major choices are before me. The term *spiritual director* is a misnomer in some ways; it implies that someone will be telling you how to organize and practice your spiritual life. Actually, a spiritual director helps you listen to the Spirit by listening to and with you and by helping you learn to observe how God is at work in your life. In *Holy Listening*, a wonderful book about spiritual direction, Margaret Guenther, Episcopal priest and spiritual director, speaks of directors as midwives, which is an appropriate image. Spiritual directors are midwives who help us pay attention to God and give birth to what is deepest in our souls.

The difference between the work of a midwife and a spiritual director, however, is that the person giving birth in a relationship that involves spiritual direction is not always aware of what is being born. Pregnant women about to give birth are quite aware of their situation, but God's desire, living deep inside us, is not always as obvious as a seven-pound baby, even when we consider ourselves to be reasonably aware spiritually. Oftentimes a good spiritual director will see glimpses of God at work in our lives before we do, which is precisely why they are invaluable in the discernment process.

A couple of years ago, I began to fantasize about making a living writing books and leading retreats and workshops. I considered it a pure fantasy, especially since I am an editor for a publishing company and regularly remind authors to have reasonable expectations about the money they will make from the sale of their books. I can't count the number of times I've counseled authors not to quit their day jobs. Still, the dream of writing and teaching kept coming to mind. It was a thought that just wouldn't disappear. So finally one day, I told my spiritual director about it and was quite surprised to find that she took the dream seriously. I'm not sure what I expected from her—perhaps to be patted on the head (metaphorically) and told to come back to reality. But she wasn't at all surprised by my desire to write and teach; I think she was just waiting for me to recognize that God was calling me in that direction.

> *Here we are, you and I, and I hope a third, Christ, is in our midst.*
>
> AELRED OF RIÉVAULX

Two years later, I'm still not ready to quit my day job—the one that pays the bills and that I like as well. But I am beginning to imagine that the day will come when I will do so. My director has never said outright that she believes this is God's call to me, and I don't think either of us knows that for sure at this point. But we both have a sense of God's possible call to enter that kind of ministry, and we watch and wait and listen together. Every once in a while she'll ask me if I've noticed how much progress I've made in being open to the possibility of that call.

Spiritual directors are good observers that way; they can help you pay more attention to where you are on the spiritual path at any given time.

Good spiritual directors have many of the same qualities we find in true soul friends: they listen very well, offer little in the way of advice, and are great at asking good and insightful questions. But while soul friends need not be further along the spiritual path than you are, a good spiritual director should be more experienced than you. That doesn't mean that the person has all the answers to your spiritual questions, but he or she should be a guide with some experience. Although spiritual directors don't have to have credentials, many today have been trained in special programs offered by seminaries and other organizations dedicated to spiritual formation or development. In the spiritual life, as in many other things, working with a guide who lacks knowledge of the spiritual terrain can be like trying to climb the Himalayas with someone who hasn't climbed them before.

Spiritual directors vary in the amount of overt guidance they choose to give. All of them will listen intently when you meet, but some also make suggestions about prayer methods or other exercises they think would help you learn to see and hear with the eyes and ears of your heart. These are usually suggestions rather than demands. Their major concern is to help you determine where God is at work in your life and what guidance you might take from that. For instance, when I first discovered that I enjoyed leading retreats and told my director about the experience, her question to me was, "Where do you see God's hand in that?" She helped me think about my love of doing retreats as a gift from God—a gift that God might desire I use.

Spiritual directors are also good observers who can help you learn to pay attention to clues about God's guidance in your life at a deeper level. One of my previous directors was excellent at helping me become aware of bodily reactions to my emotions as we talked. If I was upset or sad, he sometimes asked me where I was feeling the stress or misery. He did the same when I was excited or relaxed. Over time, I came to recognize that my stomach tightened when I was stressed and that I crossed my arms across my chest and generally pulled my body in toward my center very tightly. When I was relaxed or happy, I breathed more fully, and I didn't need to protect myself by covering my chest and abdomen with crossed arms. My body sometimes reacts to things before I am aware of what I'm feeling emotionally, but now I know that if I start crossing my arms, and my shoulders start sliding up toward my ears, and my breathing gets shallow, I should pay attention and look inside to see what's happening. That gives me a chance to pray about whatever is troublesome and ask what God might be trying to tell me about the situation in front of me.

Occasionally, a spiritual director may help you observe that you seem to be wandering from the path that God calls you to walk. This is where their experience comes into the picture. A skilled spiritual director can listen to you and to the Spirit of God and have a sense of caution when the two diverge. In the last chapter of this book, we'll explore some of the ways you can test the accuracy of your discernment for yourself, but a spiritual director who is experienced and knowing in these ways can help you ask whether or not you are truly living God's desires.

If finding a spiritual director looks helpful to you, spend some time considering what kind of person you would find helpful.

- Does it matter to you if that person is male or female? You may be most comfortable with someone of your own sex, or perhaps you find that you talk most easily with someone of the opposite sex. Personal factors related to your own history—abuse or another difficult experience—may influence your decision. You may also find that you're open to working with a person of either sex, that this isn't an issue for you.

- Does the faith background of the person make any difference to you? In the past, most spiritual directors were Catholic, but today there are spiritual directors from a variety of Christian traditions, even directors from other faith perspectives. Just be aware of any desire you might feel to have a director who comes from a particular background; God may be calling you to move in a particular direction. Again, you may find that this is not an issue for you.

- Do any other factors really matter to you? Do you want to see someone who specializes in a particular area? Directors, like everyone else, sometimes find that they are called to a particular kind of ministry. One might feel called to work with those who have been wounded by their past; another feels called to work with women, and so on. Try to be aware of a particular need that you know you'll want to address with a spiritual director.

- What is the fee for spiritual direction? Fees vary. Some directors do not charge at all, but many people who feel called to the work of spiritual direction need to charge a fee if they are to make a living doing the work

God calls them to do. Some directors charge a standard fee; others are able to offer a sliding scale. It may be useful to have a sense of what you can afford to pay a spiritual director before you begin to search for one.

Once you have looked at the questions and are ready to seek out a director, take some time in prayer to ask God's guidance in leading you to a person who is right for you.

Finding a spiritual director is not always easy, but some of the following resources will be helpful. Clergy in your area may be able to make suggestions about appropriate directors. If you live close to a seminary or retreat center, you might also check with the staff of these places; they are generally aware of those who provide direction in your geographical area. Finally, Spiritual Directors International, a professional organization of spiritual directors, based in San Francisco, has a database of thousands of directors in the United States and abroad. Check their Web site (www.sdi.org) for contact information.

Lord Jesus, merciful and patient, grant us grace, I beseech thee, ever to teach in a teachable spirit; learning along with those we teach, and learning from them whenever thou so pleasest.

CHRISTINA ROSSETTI

If possible, get the names of several possible directors to check out. A good relationship depends on the right fit between two people, and you may need to talk with two or more people to find a director who can help you walk your path. One may be more directive than another, and you may find that one style or the other suits you better. One director may have been trained in a particular approach that you find more helpful than another whose focus is elsewhere. Generally, spiritual directors will schedule either one or a limited number of sessions with you and will suggest that both of you spend that time discerning if this is the right relationship. An experienced spiritual director will be honest in telling you if someone else might be more helpful and will ask you to be honest about your own feelings about the relationship as well. As with soul friends, a good relationship with a spiritual director—one that is open to discerning God's guidance in your life—depends on both of you feeling comfortable with each other and being open and able to hear God's guidance together.

In the long run, it makes no difference whether you choose to find a soul friend or spiritual director with whom to share the details of your spiritual journey and your discernment. What matters is having a trustworthy companion who can help you stay on the path and see the way more clearly. Cassian's statement at the beginning of this chapter about God not bringing "clarification and confirmation of the truth to the heart of one who is alone" may be a bit strong. And it certainly flies in the face of the individualism of Western culture. But fundamentally Cassian is correct. Like Hero, the solitary monk, when we lack companionship along the way, we get lost too easily and become, as Cassian writes, "weak and cold in regard to the truth."

Our steps are made firm by the LORD, when he delights in our way.

PSALM 37:23

Part Three

AT
THE
CROSSROADS

In Part One, we explored some of the spiritual practices that help us live our lives focused on God's desires for us. By learning to pray regularly, practicing silence, studying, recognizing our gifts, and paying attention to the wisdom of our bodies, we prepare for and open ourselves to a deeper relationship with God on a daily basis. But chances are that many of you picked up this book because you're at a major crossroad in your life and you're looking for something more concrete. Part Three of this book is for you, whether you are just contemplating or are in the midst of a career change, geographic move, or changes in your lifestyle or relationships or circumstances.

The three chapters in this section look at the various ways big decisions can be approached so that we choose according to God's will. But if you jumped right to this section and skipped Part Two, let me encourage you to go back and read it at some point. Exploring some of the practices covered in Chapters Three through Six will enrich your experience of the ones in the next chapters, as well as your overall understanding of your place in living a part of God's will for all of us.

Once in a great while, when we face a major crossroad, we are graced with a clear and strong sense of God's will. Maybe you've had a moment or two like this when, for no apparent reason, God's guidance seems crystal clear. Once when I was getting ready for a job interview, I went to look at the bookstore I hoped to manage. I hadn't applied for the job out of any conscious sense of calling. I just wanted to move to that part of the country, and a bookstore there was in need of a manager. The day before the interview, I visited the store, trying to get a sense of its strengths and weaknesses so I could say something intelligent the next day. What I got was so much more than that; by the end of my forty-five minutes there, I had a strong sense of everything that store could be. I went to the interview the next day with a vision of the store's possibilities and was offered the job not long after that. No one was more surprised by my sense of the store than I was, and my vision for its future had nothing to do with my preparation. The strength of my dream for the store—and the overwhelming sense of that knowledge coming from outside me—left me with the clear sense that God was guiding me to that place at that moment.

Saint Ignatius, the sixteenth-century saint whose masterpiece, *The Spiritual Exercises,* still informs the study of discernment today, talks about these moments as times when God "moves and attracts the will in such a way that a devout person, without doubting or being able to doubt, carries out what was proposed."[1] These moments of flashing insight barely count as discernment, as the way seems so clear. They're wonderful when they occur, but if you're like me, you can count the number of times this has happened to you on one hand.

More often than not, we find ourselves torn between two or more options. Should we marry so-and-so? Should we take a new job that has been offered to us? Is it time to leave a relationship or a situation we've outgrown? Do we need to make a major adjustment to the priorities in our lives? We feel called to volunteer some of our time and talents, but we're not sure where they would be most helpful. There are rarely straightforward and clear answers to these kinds of questions. The practices we've already explored are helpful: praying, being silent, paying attention to one's gifts and feelings are all important in discerning God's desires for us. But more may be needed when the way ahead is hazy. We need to be very deliberate in using a wide range of skills and gifts, including our intellect, imagination, and the wisdom of others around us, in balance with our own inner knowledge and the ability to know when it is time to make a decision or wait patiently for more light.

Theory, of course, is all well and good, but the only way to really understand discernment is by doing it. Before continuing with Chapter Seven, take some time to focus on an issue in your own life that you would like to bring before God. That issue could be anything—one of those mentioned earlier or anything else for which you seek some clarity.

Once you have selected the issue to be explored, take time to make notes about your concern. Write down anything that seems relevant to the concern: background information about the issue, how and why it has arisen, what the options might be, what your feelings are about the possible options, and anything else that comes to mind. Being very clear in defining the decision at hand and possible outcomes will help you stay focused in the discernment process.

As you read the rest of Part Three, try the exercises or strategies suggested there. Be sure to take your time with them; don't rush through. The quality of

Hearing with the Heart

your effort and thoughtfulness is very important, whereas speed doesn't matter at all. Some decisions may be made easily in an afternoon or a day. For others, you may actually find that the exercises take you days or weeks to do. You'll also find that some of the exercises appeal to you or work very well for you, and others may not speak to you at all. But try to look at all of the suggestions with an open mind. Sometimes what we resist doing the most is just the thing we most need to do.

Chapter Seven

THE THOUGHTFUL AND IMAGINATIVE HEART

There must be light in the understanding as well as fervency of heart, for if a heart has heat without light, there can be nothing divine or heavenly in that heat. On the other hand, where there is light without heat, such as a head stored with notions and speculations but having a cold and unaffected heart, there can be nothing divine in that light either.[1]

JONATHAN EDWARDS

Don't think about your answer to the question I'm about to ask you. Just respond. When you have a big decision to make, which of these two methods do you use for choosing the correct path?

- I make a list of pros and cons of taking or rejecting a particular path.
- I look inward and wait for some sign of God's will for me.

There is no right or wrong answer. Both choices are correct and useful in the discernment process. Those who picked the first answer usually prefer to use logic, reason, and facts when they are trying to make a decision or choose a path. They are perfectly comfortable getting out a piece of paper and making a very clear and detailed list of the pros and cons of all the possible choices. People who choose the second response tend to look inward to their feelings and intuition for the answer. They are more likely to take long walks or sit quietly and ponder their decision, waiting for the way to become clear. Although most people use a combination of both techniques, we tend to turn first or give more credence to one over the other.

The point of the exercise is to help you gain a sense of where your own preference lies. In discernment, we need to use logic-and-reason and feelings-and-intuition in balance with each other. We must have what Jonathan Edwards calls "light in the understanding as well as fervency of heart." If you know what your first preference is, you can continue to rely on that but learn to strengthen the side that you exercise less often.

John Cassian's stories of the Desert Fathers help to illustrate why that makes a difference. Remember Hero from Chapter One? Hero's decision to jump into a well was made primarily on his sense of his own inner voices. He believed that God had called him to jump down the well and emerge unscathed as a testimony to Hero's piety. Had he exercised his reason instead of relying only on his feelings, Hero might have recalled Jesus hearing similar voices in the wilderness and rejecting them as being inconsistent with Jesus' knowledge of God. "Beloved, do not believe every spirit, but test the spirits to see whether they are from God; for many false prophets have gone out into the world," says 1 John 4:1. Hero's feelings (and ours) are all well and good, but reason is one way of testing the spirits to see if they are from God or from elsewhere.

Another of Cassian's stories demonstrates the flip side of this, that is, the danger of using logic and reason without paying attention to feelings. Two brothers on a journey through the desert are "moved by a lapse of discernment" to refuse any food except what God offers them. Starving and weak from hunger, they encounter the Mazices, a warlike race, who uncharacteristically rush forward to bring food to the two men. One of the men, "moved by discernment, accepted with joy and blessing the food offered him, as if it were the Lord Himself who was giving it. In his view the food had been made available by God himself. . . . The other man refused the food. It had been offered by man." And so the second man died of hunger.[2]

In Cassian's story, the second man starved to death because he didn't believe that God worked through dangerous barbarians. He looked only at what reason told him: the food was provided by men he feared and despised. Perhaps only angels with big white wings, bearing food, could have broken through the second man's powerful focus on what could be seen with ordinary eyes. The first man, seeing with new eyes—the eyes of the heart that knew hospitality and kindness when they saw them—understood that God can speak and act through anyone. He found God's presence in the hospitality of strangers. Perhaps he even remembered that Jesus ate with the tax collectors and other outcasts; he used his intellect as well as his feelings to discern God's invitation to take nourishment and live. But the point of Cassian's story is that the first man was moved by his feelings of joy and blessing, and so he accepted the gifts that he discerned God had sent him.

In discernment, we strive for this kind of balance between what our intellect tells us is reasonable and consistent with our understanding of the scripture's teachings about God's desires and our feelings or intuition through which we can see and hear with the heart and soul. As you read through the rest of this chapter, pay attention to your own preferences and ways of making decisions, noticing which suggestions appeal to you. Notice, too, which exercises seem pointless or boring. These are probably the ones that engage your weaker skills. Rather than just skipping them, let me encourage you to give them a try. You may be surprised at the results.

PREPARING OUR HEARTS AND MINDS

One of the most helpful guides to using reason in balance with imagination or feeling is *The Spiritual Exercises* of Saint Ignatius, written in the sixteenth-century. Ignatius' own life was full of illness and struggle. Through a series of mystical experiences and visions, Ignatius came to a deeper knowledge of God and dedicated his life to studying and teaching God's ways to others. *The Spiritual Exercises* developed out of his own experiences of discerning God's will and from his pastoral experience with teaching others his method.

In sections 179–188 of the *Exercises,* Ignatius gives us guidelines for using both reason and imagination in order to truly listen for God's call to us. His first method isolates the use of reason; his second looks at the role of imagination in discerning God's will.

Before focusing on the issue at hand, preparation is essential. If we don't prepare, we risk being like the sower of seed that Jesus speaks about in Matthew:

> A sower went out to sow. And as he sowed, some seeds fell on the path, and the birds came and ate them up. Other seeds fell on rocky ground, where they did not have much soil, and they sprang up quickly, since they had no depth of soil. But when the sun rose, they were scorched; and since they had no root, they withered away. Other seeds fell among thorns, and the thorns grew up and choked them. Other seeds fell on good soil and brought forth grain, some a hundredfold, some sixty, some thirty. (Matthew 13:3–8)

If we just jump into discernment without being clear about what the central discernment issue is and what our purpose is, chances are we'll be throwing our own seeds on poor soil where they will fail to grow. Ignatius' instructions follow next, and let me suggest that you do these exercises prayerfully. Find a time when you can do them without hurrying and a space where you can work on them without being disturbed. You can do these individually, but you can also work on them with a prayer group or others exploring discernment. Sometimes the support of a group—even your accountability to others in a community—helps you stay focused and present to the practices.

CLARIFY THE QUESTION

Step one, Ignatius wrote, is to put the matter before yourself clearly. What are you trying to discern? What is your question? The more clearly you define the question, the better your hopes of coming to a clear conclusion. If you didn't take the time to frame the question you are bringing before God (as suggested in the introduction to Part Three), now is a good time to do so. If you allow yourself to be honest and write without censoring yourself, you may be surprised by what you find. We are all expert at thinking that our concern is one thing when, in fact, it is something quite different.

Once, when I went looking for a new job and had a good possibility before me, I spent some time praying over the decision and listening to my own sense of my desires and God's. I knew before I went looking that I was unhappy with the position I currently held, but, much to my own surprise, I discovered that my impulse to find a new job was not what God was asking of me. The more I kept thinking about the new job, the more I realized that my dreams (and God's wishes) for my current position hadn't been fulfilled yet. I'd spent a great deal of time spinning my wheels, looking at the wrong issues, rather than finding a way to deal with the frustrations in my work so the dreams could be met.

In all thy ways acknowledge him, and he shall direct thy paths.

PROVERBS 3:6 (KING JAMES VERSION)

It is so simple to spend a lot of time focused on the wrong question. By putting your issue or question down in black and white or at least exploring it thoroughly in your thoughts or in conversation with others and being aware of its

background, it is possible to discover facets of the decision that have nev
curred to you. You may even discover that the question you thought was u
most in your mind isn't the right question after all.

REMAIN OPEN AND OBJECTIVE

Ignatius' second step is to remain open and objective about the possibilities. "It is necessary to keep as my objective the end for which I am created, to praise God our Lord and save my soul," he writes. "Furthermore, I ought to find myself indifferent . . . to such an extent that I am not more inclined or emotionally disposed toward making the matter proposed than letting go of it, nor more toward letting it go than taking it."[3] In other words, we practice openness to God's desires, to putting that at the forefront of our discernment process and let our willingness to follow God be our guide.

Being indifferent toward the outcome, however, is far easier said than done. Rarely are we truly indifferent or equally willing to take either or any of the paths before us. Imagine choosing between two jobs or deciding to marry or stay single. We are not likely to be without a preference for one outcome or the other; rather, we are like the contestant on a game show who wants God to pick door number one. But as much as possible, try to remain open to all possibilities. You never know what bit of evidence may tip the scales in an unexpected way.

Parker Palmer, the wonderful educator and writer we encountered in Chapter Four, for instance, tells the story of trying to decide if he should accept an offer to become president of a college—a prestigious job and a great honor. As he explored his options and his motivations for accepting or rejecting the job, he finally discovered that what he really wanted, more than the job, was to have his picture in the newspaper with the word *president* under it. Realizing that he didn't really want the job as much as the prestige, he withdrew his name from consideration.[4] Palmer's experience is far from unique; this happens to all of us on one occasion or another. If he hadn't been open to the possibility that this wasn't the right job for him, however, he might have been a college president—and probably an unhappy one.

PRAY FOR GOD'S GUIDANCE

The third step in Ignatius' system is to pray to God to move our will so that we can know what we should do. We don't rely on our own resources in discernment, but we pray for God's guidance and the will to follow it. This isn't as easy as it sounds; it is easy to say a prayer and ask for guidance and the will to follow through, but it can be difficult to put aside our own willfulness and desire for a specific outcome. When you're ready to do that, however, take a little time to sit quietly, place your concerns or options before God verbally or silently, and ask for guidance. If you're uncomfortable coming up with your own prayer, the Episcopal Book of Common Prayer has a wonderful one to use: "O God . . . Grant us in all our (my) doubts and uncertainties, the grace to ask what you would have us (me) to do, that the Spirit of wisdom may

Search me, O God, and know my heart; test me and know my thoughts.

PSALM 139:23

save us (me) from all false choices, and that in your light we (I) may see light, and in your straight path may not stumble; through Jesus Christ our Lord. Amen."

There are lots of other printed prayers for this kind of situation as well, and you'll find some of them on the pages of this book. But you should also feel perfectly free to make up your own prayer. Whatever prayer you choose to say, you'll probably find that you need to say it over and over again as you continue to try to discern what you should be doing. Much as we would like to have God deliver a verdict just as we ask for it, that rarely happens. I've prayed over some decisions for months before sensing any clear guidance from God.

REASON: MAKING A LIST AND
CHECKING IT TWICE

All three of the steps just described, part of Ignatius' first method, help prepare us for a balanced discernment process. Next, Ignatius asks us to focus specifically on our reasoning skills:

> I should consider and reason out how many advantages or benefits accrue to myself from having [what is proposed] all of them solely for the praise of God our Lord and the salvation of my soul; and on the contrary I should similarly consider the disadvantages and dangers in having it.[5]

In other words, Ignatius suggests that we make a pro-and-con list for the choices before us. Some questions you might consider while making that list include these:

What will be gained in choosing each of the paths before you?

What will be lost by rejecting any of the choices?

How do the choices benefit others?

In what ways do the choices inconvenience or disrupt the lives of others?

What excites you most about the options? What do you look forward to?

What would you dislike if you picked one path or the other?

What are your motivations for choosing one option or another?

Ignatius asks us to do this with love of God and our salvation as the basis of our list. Perhaps a contemporary way to think about this instruction is to make your list by considering what actions will put you in the best relationship with God possible. What do you think God most desires from and for you? Unless we are quite spiritually mature, however, and our own will matches our sense of God's desires for us, this is nearly impossible. Just be honest with your answers, and try not to censor yourself as you make the list. Write down everything that comes to mind, whether you think it reflects well on you or not. If one of the pros is that one job is more prestigious or pays more than another— things you seek for your own satisfaction rather than God's glory—write it down anyway. I find that getting these kinds of things down on paper helps me move past them and get to more meaty parts of my list quickly. God knows what is in your heart whether you put it on paper or not. But if your only pro turns out to be that the job will heighten your visibility, you may have your answer without having to discern any further, just as Parker Palmer did.

May God, who rules over all the world, give to you wisdom, intelligence, understanding, knowledge of his judgments, with patience.

LETTER OF BARNABAS 21

Hearing with the Heart

Ignatius' fourth step is to examine that list you made and "see to which side reason more inclines." These last two steps of Ignatius' focus on reason alone. It is impossible to separate reason from feeling completely, but Ignatius asks us to do that as much as we can and put feelings or imagination aside for the moment. What Ignatius does not address is the question of what he considers reasonable. What seems reasonable to you may seem completely unreasonable to me. Is it reasonable, for instance, to take a new job that pays much less than your current position? To buy a home in a community that locates you someplace you want to live but requires a lengthy commute each day? To form a lifelong partnership with someone you love but who is very different from you? Maybe yes and maybe no. There are no definitive answers to these questions. You will have to be the judge of what is reasonable by your standards, the standards of others who may be affected by your decision, and finally, by your sense of what furthers your relationship with God, what is consistent with the gifts you believe God gave you, and with your sense of God's desires for your wholeness.

To Ignatius' method, I would add a suggestion about paying attention to your own experience of writing and reviewing the pro-and-con lists. Do you find yourself writing many responses on one side of the list or the other? Do you have any sense of energy or lethargy related to the pros or the cons? What options seem to get your energy or creative juices flowing as you think about them? Pay attention as well to the weight you give to your responses; not all will be weighted equally. Any single entry in the pro or con column might be a "deal breaker" or a "deal maker." And be sure to listen to your body's wisdom about which path to take as you consider and make your list. Do you find yourself getting very anxious, for instance, or does a sense of peace descend on you as you make your lists? Are you finding that your stomach tightens, your back tenses, or a headache develops, or are you filled with a sense of energy and enthusiasm? These kinds of bodily clues sometimes indicate what we need to do long before we recognize the answer with our intellect.

Finally, there are times when we know what we think we should do, but the size and scope of following the path ahead overwhelms us. We're thinking of adopting a child, and the process itself, not to mention all the changes in our lives, looms large. We feel called to start a business of our own but can't imagine making it through the maze of paperwork, financial material, and other details. We're thinking about leaving a long-term relationship but can't figure out how we're going to manage on our own. Although there are definitely emotional factors to consider in these situations and others that may confront us, it is easy to put all the different parts of what lies ahead together into one huge ball that rolls right over us.

If you have a clear sense that one option is right for you, but you're feeling overwhelmed at the thought of actually taking that path, spend some time breaking the whole into its various parts. When you are looking at a path that is new for you, some research may even be helpful; it might give you a clearer sense of what you would have to do along the way. If you're thinking about beginning your own business, for instance, read some books on the subject, talk to some business advisers and others who have started their own business, and develop your own business plan. If you're thinking of adoption, familiarize yourself with the process and make a realistic plan for working through it. Though leaving a long-term relationship is not as methodical as the other two examples, you can still make a list of the support systems you will need and the strategies you can use to deal with the emotional, financial, and other issues. Consulting books and professionals may help you overcome the financial or emotional obstacles that are keeping you in a relationship that isn't working anymore.

What you may discover in the process of researching and planning is that the way ahead is not as impossible as it first seemed. A friend of mine who wanted to start his own business but who was anxious about the lack of security in working for himself, finally began to read books on business planning; he talked to accountants and insurance companies and others who walked him through the maze of decisions that would need to be made. Using all this information, he was able to figure out how much money he really needed to live on and create a business plan that he thought could provide that income. The life to which he felt called but which overwhelmed him for a year or so finally became a reality.

> *Do not be conformed to this world, but be transformed by the renewing of your minds, so that you may discern what is the will of God—what is good and acceptable and perfect.*
>
> ROMANS 12:2

At this point, you are ready to take the final step in Ignatius' first method for making a sound discernment, which is to take your conclusions to God in prayer and, with open heart, ask for confirmation or guidance that your discernment is correct.

Confirmation is attained, in Ignatius' system, through a sense of moving toward or away from God when we bring our decision before God. We experience either feelings of consolation or of desolation. These are often difficult to describe and tricky to understand, and a guide, such as a spiritual friend or director, can be very helpful.

Feelings of consolation are those that cause the soul to be "inflamed with the love of its Creator," says Ignatius. A sense of peacefulness, joy, love, or feeling at one with all that exists, surprises, and delights are examples of feelings of consolation. But feelings of consolation may also include tears or even anger, particularly when they are in response to personal or societal injustices. A sense of sorrow for past errors or wrongs we have done and a desire to be back in alignment with God's desires for us may be experiences of consolation. Feelings of consolation always pull us toward and into a deeper relationship with God. The experience of consolation as we pray may be a good indication that we have made a decision that is in alignment with God's will. Ignatius warns us, though, that feelings of consolation are not always signs of accurate discernment. Like Hero, in Chapter One, we can be fooled by our own feelings. We'll look some more at this in the final chapter of the book, but in many cases feelings of consolation suggest that we are on the right path.

Feelings of desolation, in contrast, include "darkness of soul, turmoil within it, an impulsive motion toward low and earthly things, or disquiet from various agitations and temptations,"[6] according to Ignatius. These feelings separate us from God and include feelings of listlessness, boredom, unhappiness, anxiety, and hopelessness, frustration, or anger. Unfortunately, many of these feelings—even the sense of God's absence—can be experiences of depression as easily as ones of desolation. An experienced guide can help you figure out the difference.

Feelings of consolation and desolation are experienced in the body as well. Feelings of consolation may be accompanied by renewed energy, by a release of anxiety or strain that you have been holding in one or more parts of your body, by a sense of relaxation and peacefulness. Feelings of desolation tend to bring about the opposite bodily sensations. Your energy may be suddenly sapped, or you might find tightness or pain creeping into one or more areas in your body. Your bodily reactions may differ, but you will be able to identify which ones connote a deepening connection to God versus those that come from a sense of separation from God's desires for you. As you pray for confirmation of your decision, try to pay attention to what is happening in your body as well as what is going on emotionally for you.

As you get a sense of your feelings, whether of consolation or desolation, it is important to confirm those feelings through other methods and with the help of other people. It is all too easy to feel that you are on the right path but be mistaken, or to feel you are going down the wrong road and be mistaken about that, too. So it is wise not to rely solely on the use of reason—or any of the other skills or gifts you'll read about in this book. Pay attention to what you are thinking, feeling, and hearing with your heart in all of these exercises; if they all point you in the same direction and if others confirm what you are sensing, you can feel more confident about the direction in which you sense God calls you.

IGNATIUS' SECOND METHOD: JUST MY IMAGINATION

Ignatius' second method of making a good discernment has us turning away from reason for a while and using our imagination to explore the options before us. It is impossible to completely turn off our reasoning, but this method gives the imagination free reign as much as possible without limiting it to what seems reasonable or even feasible. You can always deal with "reality" later. This is the time to explore what your heart desires and what your life might look like if you followed that yearning.

As with his first method, Ignatius begins by reminding us to approach the decision clearly, with a solid sense of the issue to be explored. Then, with the love of God uppermost in our thoughts, we try to practice indifference to the outcome. Put another way, we practice openness to the various possibilities, and we ask for God's guidance. Of course, this kind of indifference or openness is difficult. One approach to indifference is to recognize that you don't actually have to make a decision right now, that you don't have to be indifferent at the point of actual decision making. Try to suspend whatever desires you have just for the time being, knowing that you can pick them up again later.

Once we have prepared ourselves in this way, Ignatius suggests that we imagine three different scenarios. First, imagine that someone comes to you with the same dilemma you face and asks your advice. You can do this exercise silently in your head, or you may find it useful to write it out in the form of a dialogue between you and the other person. Most of us jump quickly and easily to giving advice. But take some time to explore and then really listen to what this person has to say about his or her situation. What questions would you ask, and how would that imaginary person answer you? Try to get a sense of how you think this person is feeling and how that influences the advice you would give. Keeping uppermost in your mind your desire for the person to choose the dream of God, what path would you recommend taking?

I love Ignatius' wisdom—or perhaps humor—in proposing this exercise, because it is so easy for us to tell others what they should do. How often has the path a friend should take seemed perfectly clear to you, while your friend remains mired in indecision? But Ignatius tricks us just a bit with his next direction: "Then, doing the same for myself, I will keep the rule which I have set up for another."[7] So much for advice! It is far easier to give sage counsel to others than it is to listen to it ourselves.

Next, Ignatius asks us to imagine ourselves on our own deathbed, looking back at the decision we are now trying to make. What path do you wish you had chosen? Another way of doing this is to imagine how your own obituary will appear someday and what you hope it will say. This is a little like placing yourself in the classic Dickens story, *A Christmas Carol,* in which Ebenezer Scrooge looks back over his life and determines that he has made poor choices, ones that he amends before it is truly too late. Everyone knew that Scrooge was a miser and a mean man, but he was either oblivious to that fact or simply didn't care about what others thought. Only when Scrooge saw and felt the effects of his actions on others and himself in his dreams did he change his ways.

> *Many peoples shall come and say, "Come, let us go up to the mountain of the LORD, to the house of the God of Jacob; that he may teach us his ways and that we may walk in his paths."*
>
> ISAIAH 2:3

Pretend that you are Scrooge dreaming or that you are on your own deathbed. Look back on your past, your present and the decision before you, and your future, having chosen a particular path. What do you think your life will look like, having pursued one of the options before you? What would it look like if you took the other path? Pay close attention to how you feel emotionally and physically as you imagine these scenarios. Does one give you a greater sense of energy, enthusiasm, or peacefulness (feelings of consolation)? Or does one of them cause tension, tightness in your body, anxiety, anger, or resentment (feelings of desolation)? If you're looking back from your deathbed, which path do you think will be the one that brings you closest to living as God's body in this world?

Finally, Ignatius suggests that we consider ourselves on the final judgment day. We don't often think or speak of this in mainstream churches today, other than when we recite the Apostle's Creed. If you find it difficult to imagine the final judgment day or if this scenario raises troublesome images of a judgmental and punishing God, think instead of being face-to-face with God, who loves you, reviewing the choices you have made. Try to imagine what you would say to God and how it would feel to review the choices you have made. Of the choices before you, is there one that you would find easiest to speak to God about? Which would you rather not discuss with God? Which path do you think will bring you into a deeper relationship or responsiveness to God? Finally, which option do you believe is the clearest choice for you as God's loving agent in the world?

How precious is your steadfast love, O God! For with you is the fountain of life; in your light we see light.

PSALM 36:7A, 9

You may find it helpful to write your answers to these questions in the form of a dialogue with God. As with the exercises described previously, pay attention to the feelings, hopes, desires, and dreams that arise as you explore these imaginary moments, as well as to any anger, frustration, or distress.

After exploring these three imaginary scenarios and noticing your feelings and bodily responses, you may have a clearer sense of the path to choose. Ignatius recommends that we follow the same procedure we did with the exercise using reason and bring this discernment to God with an openness of heart and mind, asking for confirmation or re-direction.

The genius in Ignatius' system and perhaps the reason it has endured for so long is the balance of feelings and reason his exercises provide. We all have both of these, but many of us tend to use one more easily than the other. Ignatius asks us to use both and to develop, as Jonathan Edwards' quote at the beginning of the chapter states so wonderfully, a heart that has both the light of understanding and one that is filled with heat and passion as well.

Chapter Eight

HEARTS TOGETHER

The spiritual responsibility to discern whether the source of our inner prompt-
ings is in our true or false self, to grasp the direction of changes and what they
require of us, is especially weighty at the turning points of our lives. At those
moments when the inner movement of our growth intersects with the cry of
need in the world, we require not only the disciplined practice of prayer,
but the loving and discerning support of spiritual community as well.[1]

PATRICIA LORING

I'm not sure I would have believed it if
I hadn't actually been present. In a course given by Parker Palmer, we were
divided into small groups and taught a method for a group to help one of its own
members in the task of discernment; we had the afternoon to try it out. For several

hours, a young man who had volunteered to be the "focus person" sat before us while we all listened to him and for the voice of God regarding a new direction for his life. He'd been contemplating a possibility for a year or more but couldn't discern whether he should stay where he was or launch out in a new—and riskier—direction. He had been stuck for a long time. But by the end of the afternoon, he came to see that he was being invited to try the new direction. He felt at peace with that decision and empowered to move ahead.

I will give thanks to the LORD with my whole heart, in the assembly of the upright, in the congregation.

PSALM 111:1, THE BOOK OF COMMON PRAYER

Because the young man lived many states away from me, I never saw him or heard from him after that class ended, but I'd be surprised to hear that he didn't take action on what he'd discerned that day. I've been part of other groups using this same method since that time; I was even the focus person once, when I was confused about the direction of my own life. It isn't a cure-all answer for every difficult decision, but I've seen this particular method make a great difference in my own life and in the lives of others.

It was not amazing, of course, that the young man came to a sense of clarity about his heart's desires and the direction in which God called him. What was amazing was that someone who had been confused about this issue for many months became clear in the course of an afternoon, sitting with a group of people he had known for four days and without anyone offering a single word of advice. Perhaps it is astonishing, in and of itself, that no advice was given that afternoon. Refraining from advising another doesn't sound all that difficult, but it was one of the hardest things I've ever had to do.

Hearing with the Heart

The method Parker Palmer taught us—a discernment technique known as the clearness committee—was one he had learned from the Society of Friends or, as they are more commonly known, Quakers. Of all the faith perspectives I've come across, the Society of Friends offers one of the most helpful understandings of the importance of valuing the individual perception of God's will in balance with the community's. Everyone, according to the Quakers, has access to God and to God's truth, so each person's experience of that is important and is to be taken seriously. God is often experienced by "waiting on the Lord," listening for God, usually in silence, either by one's self or within the worship service, known as the meeting. Quakers experience God in other ways as well, but they place great value on silence and expectant waiting for God's word to become known.

> *Let me hear what God the LORD will speak, for he will speak peace to his people, to his faithful, to those who turn to him in their hearts.*
>
> PSALM 85:8

They also believe that even though, theoretically, all of God's truth is available to each person, some people, in practice, understand or have a deeper experience of that truth than others do. A "measure" of truth is bestowed on each individual. "If we are faithful to our measure of Light,"

> *For where two or three are gathered in my name, I am there among them.*
>
> MATTHEW 18:20

writes Quaker historian Howard Brinton, "we shall be guided up to God, and up to a greater measure of the Truth."[2] Because it is unlikely that anyone has the full measure of Truth, Quakers practice communal discernment regularly, relying on that and on "coming to unity" (sometimes referred to as consensus) for making decisions rather than voting or using other systems that promote winners and losers. I'm not necessarily recommending that you go around to all of your friends, family, and spiritual community seeking consensus every time you are struggling with a concern or decision. Still, Quaker methods have a lot to teach us about balancing what we, as individuals, feel is God's will for us with what others in our community understand to be God's truth. And listening to the community is a critical safeguard against fooling ourselves about God's desires for us.

THE CLEARNESS COMMITTEE

Clearness committees are not for ordinary, everyday concerns and discernment. For one thing, they require too much work and energy from too many people. But in the midst of a discernment that feels major in your life or one that you've considered for some time without finding clarity, this particular method can be enormously helpful. "A clearness committee meets with a person who is unclear on how to proceed in a keenly felt concern or dilemma, hoping that it can help this person reach clarity," writes Jan Hoffman in a pamphlet describing the process. "It assumes that each of us has an Inner Teacher who can guide us and therefore that the answers sought are within the person seeking clearness. It also assumes that a group of caring friends can serve as channels of divine guidance in drawing out that Inner Teacher."[3] Just as spiritual friends and spiritual directors can help us get off the treadmill of rehashing the same thoughts repeatedly without coming to conclusion, the clearness committee, when functioning properly, can do the same thing. Like spiritual companions, the clearness committee exists to help the focus person—the one asking for clarity—to listen to God. "The purpose of committee members is not to give advice or to 'fix' the situation; they are there to listen without prejudice or judgment, to help clarify alternatives, to help communication if necessary, and to provide emotional support as an individual seeks to find 'truth and the right course of action.'"[4]

A clearness committee, in Quaker history, began as something closer to a "clearance" committee. This group met with individuals, such as couples to be married, and it made sure that everything was in order before the individual's or couple's request came before the entire meeting—the congregation. The committee dealt largely with outward issues rather than inward or spiritual ones. They ensured that everything was in order legally, that all relevant information was available, and so on. But in the 1960s, this clearance committee began to evolve into a process of discernment for things that were deemed too personal to bring to the meeting as a whole. Its evolving purpose has been to help individuals discern or recognize the inward calling of God in their lives and to offer support during that process.

> *O, let thy sacred will*
> *All thy delight in me fulfil!*
> *Let me not think an action*
> *mine own way,*
> *But as thy love shall sway,*
> *Resigning up the rudder*
> *to thy skill.*
>
> GEORGE HERBERT

THE CLEARNESS COMMITTEE PROCESS

The procedure for conducting a clearness committee is deceptively simple. What is difficult about the process is not the "hows" of doing it but the need to resist the "wholly human urge to share, to instruct, or to straighten people out," as Quaker author Patricia Loring writes. So the first step in creating a group to serve as your clearness committee is to seek out five or six people who are able to resist these tendencies—people who seem to be good listeners and are able to refrain from being judgmental. Some diversity within the group can also be helpful. It is important to involve both men and women, as well as some people who are "thinkers" and others who are "feelers," people with a variety of perspectives, and people whom you trust to keep your comments confidential. Each of these people needs to agree to meet as a group for at least one meeting that is two or three hours in length, with the possibility of additional meetings if needed.

O heavenly Father, the author and fountain of all truth, the bottomless sea of all understanding, send, we beseech thee, thy Holy Spirit into our hearts, and lighten our understandings with the beams of thy heavenly grace.

NICHOLAS RIDLEY

Once you have selected the group, choose a time and meeting place and make sure that everyone is available to attend. Plan to hold the meeting in a comfortable place where you can meet without interruptions from people, phones, or other distractions. In advance of the meeting, ask one member of the committee to be the "clerk," that is, the person who opens and closes the meeting and keeps everything on track. Ask another person to be the "recorder" if you wish. This person keeps notes about what questions are asked and gives you these notes so you have something to refer to later. Also, in advance of the meeting, ask the clerk to distribute information about how the meeting will be run.

As with the Ignatian method of discernment, take time to write a description of your question or concern. If you already did this at the beginning of Part Three of this book, you're set. If not, take time to do that now. Include any relevant background information that the committee needs to know. Make sure everyone on the committee has a copy of this well in advance of the meeting so they can read it and pray over it.

At the meeting itself, the clerk begins by reminding the committee about the guidelines and making sure everyone understands that anything said during this time remains confidential. Committee members are not to repeat anything that is said during the meeting. There is to be no mention of the conversation again after the meeting or any attempt to find out if the focus person has followed up on what they discerned during the meeting. If there are no questions about the method or other details, the clerk begins the meeting with a period of silence. Writes Quaker author Patricia Loring:

> This is not the "moment of silence" which is a mere nod in passing to the divine. Nor is it a time for organizing one's thoughts. This is a time for what has been called recollection: for an intentional return to the Center, to give over one's own firm views, to place the outcome in the hands of God, to ask for a mind and heart as truly sensitive to and accepting of nuanced intimations of God's will as of overwhelming evidences of it.[5]

The silence is broken by the focus person, who restates the concern before the group when he or she is ready.

The majority of the meeting time is spent in asking questions of the focus person and listening to his or her answers. This is the hard part! Committee members may ask any question that seems appropriate to them, though the focus person is entirely free to choose not to answer a given question if it makes him or her uncomfortable. But the questions must be honest questions rather than statements or leading questions. Comments such as "Don't you think it would work if you . . . ?" or "Want to know what I did when I faced the same situation . . . ?" are not permitted. Questions should be brief, without a lengthy explanation about why you're asking. "The ground rule of questions only is simple," writes Parker Palmer, "but its implications are demanding. It means no advice, no overidentification . . . no handing off the problem to someone else . . . no suggestions of books to read, techniques to use, meditations to practice, therapists to see."[6] It sounds very simple, but based on my own experience and that of others, I can tell you that this is the hardest part of the process. We love nothing more than to offer each other advice and counsel. I had no idea how much I loved doing that until I had my first experience as a committee member. Because it is so easy for us to jump in with answers or advice, the clerk (or anyone else who notices that this is happening) is asked to gently steer the conversation back to honest questions whenever necessary.

The focus person may answer the questions in any way he or she chooses, and the next question should not be asked until the focus person is finished speaking. We all have a habit of formulating our response to something as we listen to someone, which frequently prevents us from really listening. In the clearness committee, as no response is expected of us, we can let go of the need to come up with a clever response and simply listen to the focus person. The meeting time should be filled with what Patricia Loring calls "the comfortable silence that flows gracefully around questions and answers." Her description of this kind of silence and response, a truly countercultural one for us, is helpful:

To truly enter into this attentive, prayerful listening is to let go of displaying our preparedness; our rapidity of thought, analysis or response; our intelligence or profundity. It is to allow the questions and the answers to sink into us in the silence which follows them; to sink into the questions and answers; to wait on whatever will arise from the depths, in confidence that . . . when it is right and necessary, utterance will be given without our having fashioned and honed it in advance. We trust in the availability of God's guidance in ways that may be unexpected, even surprising.[7]

As the questions begin to slow down toward the end of the two or three hours together, the clerk should ask the focus person how he or she wants to proceed. The focus person may wish to continue with questions but may also choose to listen to the reflections of the committee at this time. Even now, giving advice or interpreting or attaching values such as happiness or sadness is forbidden. The reflections of the group assembled—what Parker Palmer and others call mirroring—should take the form of pointing out things that the focus person might not have noticed in his or her own responses and bodily reactions. Committee members might point out how weary the focus person sounded when discussing a particular path versus the energy in her voice and body when she explored another. They act as a "mirror" for the focus person, reflecting back their observations about what was said and what they saw.

Before the meeting concludes, the focus person may also choose to share his or her reflections on any clarity reached or may request another meeting to continue exploring the concern at hand. This isn't a Hollywood film in which everything magically resolves at the end, though significant clarity is often reached in one meeting. When that isn't the case, this is a good time to schedule another session.

I've found this process to be enormously helpful in my own life and discernments. About ten years ago, I spent about a month trying to decide if I should be a youth leader in a church. I had been a youth leader before and loved the time I spent with the high school group. At the same time, I wasn't sure I really wanted to be a youth leader at that particular time in my life, but I wasn't sure why not. It seemed like something I "should" return to. As I explored my sense of what was calling me, I finally realized that I was looking for community in a way that had worked for me before, but it wasn't what I needed at that particular time. The issue at hand was really one of being brave enough to find a new way of developing a community for myself in this new church, not whether I should become a youth leader. But without the questions of the clearness committee, the ones that helped me focus on what my heart really desired and what role I was called to take

> *Lord, help me today to realize that you will be speaking to me through the events of the day, through people, through things, and through all creation. Give me ears, eyes and heart to perceive you, however veiled your presence may be. Give me insight to see through the exterior of things to the interior truth. Give me your Spirit of discernment. O Lord, you know how busy I must be this day. If I forget you, do not forget me. Amen.*
>
> ADAPTED FROM JACOB ASTLEY

Hearing with the Heart

in that church, I might have just done what I thought I should do instead of pursuing what God desired I do.

ONE NOTE OF CAUTION

As I have said often in this book, discernment is a rewarding process, but it also has its dangers; one of those is to beware of the group mentality. In situations as unremarkable as on a school playground, we see the kind of tyranny that a group of children can exercise over those who are not part of the "in" crowd. Our own history is full of cases, such as the internment of Japanese Americans during World War II, when groups in power have exercised control over others in damaging ways.

Even the Quakers, who value the individual's and community's sense of God's call so highly, discovered that abuse is possible in discernment. Early in their history, the Quakers discovered that some individuals seemed to be more adept at discerning God's movement within the community than others. These people, known as elders, were asked to exercise their gift by helping others in the meeting (the congregation) to discern their own callings and to help the meeting as a whole recognize true callings, or leadings, as the Quakers call them. Unfortunately, over time some elders began exercising a legalistic authority over the meeting and shifted from observations of the Inner Light within each person to outward signs of faithfulness. As Patricia Loring notes, "Unity in the Spirit was judged by conformity to a code of dress. Commitment to God was brought into question by interest in the arts. Frivolity was ascertained by the length of bonnet strings."[8]

It is as easy for a community to fool itself, even one as spiritually grounded as the Society of Friends, as it is for individuals to fool themselves. Perhaps this is especially true in communities that are committed to deeply felt causes, where the group insists on conformity to a particular line of thought. I've also seen it happen all too often in retreats, where a group leader intentionally induces emotional breakdowns of participants in the mistaken belief that this is a healthy release of the individual's or group's stresses; those who refuse to fall apart emotionally are accused (tacitly or silently) of being distant, dishonest in their feelings, or otherwise disruptive to the group process.[9]

There are many cases, too, when a group's insistence on a particular direction or idea comes from the best of intentions. Sometimes their ideas are in support of an important cause that they feel strongly about. At other times, the majority of a group becomes convinced that they know The Answer—something they think is truly helpful—and they push for what they want. Many times this is well intentioned, and they may, indeed, have the right answer. But an unwillingness to listen to alternative ideas prevents proper discernment for the group as a whole and for the individual who is in doubt.

Although this is an unpleasant topic, it is important to recognize that any process, even one as helpful as the clearness committee, can be abused. It is important to recognize the signs of an abusive group in order to extricate yourself from the process if nothing else. Danger signs include

- A whole clearness committee or one or more members who ask questions that are either much too personal or that seem to be coming from their own curiosity instead of addressing the focus person's concern

- An insistence, either overt or subtle, that the focus person answer questions that she or he finds uncomfortable

- Advice giving, or a sense that the committee is trying to push the focus person in a particular direction that cannot be controlled by the clerk of the meeting

- A focus person's feeling of anxiety

Any desire to flee from the group or any bodily symptoms of distress should be attended to. Even though some anxiety about discussing your concerns with a group is natural, excessive distress that doesn't ease as the conversation goes along may mean this is the wrong group for you.

These kinds of signs do not necessarily indicate malicious intent by a group. We are, all of us, fallible human beings who sometimes form ourselves into fallible committees and groups. But intentional or not, this kind of group experience is unlikely to be helpful in your own discernment.

❀ ❀ ❀

Luckily, these kinds of difficult group experiences are not the norm. I have been a part of several clearness committees and have found all of them to be powerful in discerning God's guidance for myself or for others who requested help using this method. It is difficult to describe how supportive a clearness committee can be, especially when you are deeply conflicted about making a decision or choosing a direction. Knowing that others walk with you, that they support your search for God's will in your life, and that they care whether you find it or not can make all the difference in finding God's desires for you and in being confident of that discernment.

Chapter Nine

THE ENGAGED HEART

God grant me the wisdom of patience. Let me see clearly this day the difference between patience and cowardice, between patience and fear, between patience and weakness. At my moments of confusion, give me the insight needful for Thy purpose in me. Teach me that my fear of impatience may be a mere indulgence. There are some things in the presence of which I dare not be patient lest they destroy and render evil even the good intent and the holy will. God grant me the wisdom of patience.[1]

HOWARD THURMAN

There was once a very patient man who wanted to win the lottery. He was a man of faith, so for many years he asked God to help him win. Day by day, month after month, year in and year out he prayed to God to bring him the winning lottery ticket. After many years of patient waiting, this man finally got tired and frustrated. "God, I have prayed to you for years about this. I have been faithful to you all my life. Why haven't you helped me win the lottery after all this time?" he demanded. He got an answer from God immediately: "It would help if you would buy a ticket!"

That's an old joke, and I'm not sure that bothering God about winning the lottery is the best use of our time, or God's, but the joke makes a great point. There is a time for patience and attentiveness and a time to act. Patience, attentiveness, and faithfulness are all important when we're listening for God's desires. The faithful man's prayers about his heart's desire to win the lottery were legitimate. (We could give him the benefit of the doubt and assume he wanted the money in order to help others.) Fundamentally, his patient waiting was well advised. Still, if we wait patiently but don't really listen with our hearts, if we require God to put Moses' burning bush in front of us before we act, we will miss all sorts of opportunities. Maybe the faithful man could have won the lottery twenty times over if he had just listened earlier and bought some tickets. If we never act on what we have heard with the ears of our hearts, God's work might never be done—at least not by us.

Think about your own preferences for a moment. Do you like things organized, scheduled, neatly laid out? Are you more comfortable after a decision has been made than while you're considering what should be done? Or do you like lots of open options to consider? Are you someone who prefers to go with the flow rather than follow a set schedule? These questions bring out extremes, such as people like Felix and Oscar in the play and television show "The Odd Couple"; most of us fall somewhere between the two. But we often have a preference—

slight or large—for one end of the spectrum over the other, and that preference affects our discernment process. If you're more comfortable making decisions, you might try to rush God or just tell God what you plan to do rather than listen patiently and attentively. And if you're a person who likes open options, you might find it hard to settle on a course of action that eliminates other possibilities, even when you've heard God clearly with your heart. Both ways of being have advantages and disadvantages; neither is inherently good or bad. But knowing how you operate or where you are most comfortable can help you use the advantages of your own preference and avoid some of the disadvantages. This can be particularly important when you are trying to discern God's will at a major crossroad in your life.

Think of it this way. I take the train into and out of New York City several times a year and find myself in line to buy tickets at Amtrak. Waiting in line involves patience. You can't cut in front of someone else. There isn't much to do, although you might get into the occasional conversation with someone else in line. Mostly you just wait your turn. When you're the first person in line, you stare at a sign something like this: PLEASE WAIT. And suddenly the sign changes to one that indicates the gate where an employee is free to help you. At that point, you'd better move or you risk the ire of all the people who are standing behind you. There is a time for patience in this process; you just wait patiently until the time is right to do something. And when the light comes on, you move forward. Moving forward before it is our turn and our time to do so would be dangerous. Not taking action when it is time is equally problematic. Of course, knowing when to wait and when to move at the Amtrak station isn't all that difficult. Knowing when to be patient and when to act in the discernment process is trickier.

A PATIENT HEART

Patience is not a word we hear all that often today. With cell phones, pagers, e-mail, and instant messages, not to mention the old-fashioned telephone and fax, we are accustomed to fast responses and instant gratification. Letters have become passé; we call them snail mail now. Waiting three to five days for something to be delivered is nearly intolerable. It stretches our patience to the limit. Some of us, in the midst of the discernment process, wish that God would "get with it" and modernize a bit. An e-mail, fax, or a quick call to our cell phone with The Answer would be most welcome. Truth be told, when I'm trying to decipher God's will at an important moment in my life, I'd much prefer to set up an appointment to discuss the facts and make a decision—say, next Tuesday at two o'clock—than to listen patiently for days, weeks, or even for months. I can't bear to contemplate waiting longer than months. I would have been one of the Israelites who grumbled at Moses and God out in the desert after leaving slavery in Egypt. I would have been right in there with the folks who wanted to know where the water and food were and when the journey was going to end.

Our soul waits for the LORD; he is our help and shield. Our heart is glad in him, because we trust in his holy name.

PSALM 33:20–21

I waited patiently for the LORD; he inclined to me and heard my cry.

PSALM 40:1

And I'm not alone in struggling with patience. Busyness has become epidemic in our world. More than that, being busy and breathless all the time is practically a status symbol. Busy people have no time to wait; they're too important for that. I remember selling books after a lecture once, with crowds of people trying to buy the speaker's books. One man, an important person who had won the Pulitzer Prize in his younger years, simply stepped in front of everyone in line and thrust his money at me while I was working with another customer. He believed that his needs came before everyone else's. Being busy and too important to wait indicates that we are in control. "We assume we are most fully human," writes philosopher David Harned, "when we are in control, actors and not acted upon, subjects rather than objects."[2] We prefer being God to being one of God's creatures. We would rather set God's agenda for God than wait patiently for God's agenda to be revealed.

Despite the fact that we're hyper-aware of the lack of patience in today's world, it isn't a new problem. In the middle of the nineteenth century, Danish philosopher Søren Kierkegaard observed the same kind of impatience.

> When a man is active early and late "for the sake of the Good," storming about noisily and restlessly, hurling himself into time . . . then the masses think what he himself imagines, that he is inspired. And yet he is at the other pole from that. . . . He cannot, he will not, humbly understand that the Good can get on without him.[3]

It seems that busyness, which is actually a form of pridefulness, has been more popular than patience for some time. But Kierkegaard recommended something we've already explored: pausing and paying attention. "Pausing is not a sluggish repose. Pausing is also movement. It is the inward movement of the heart. To pause is to deepen oneself in inwardness. But merely going further is to go straight in the direction of superficiality."[4]

But for those of us—and I include myself in this category—who feel very comfortable making decisions and getting things done, waiting on a sense of God's will for us is extremely difficult, especially when we have a major decision to make. Being undecided feels like living in limbo. As Methodist writer Rueben Job notes, "True discernment calls us beyond the well-tended gardens of conventional religious wisdom to the margin between the known and the unknown, the domesticated and the wild."[5] If we're really good at coming to closure when confronted with a dilemma, we're probably pretty uncomfortable with living in the marginal time; we like the domesticated a whole lot better than the wild.

Let nothing disturb thee,
Nothing affright thee;
All things are passing;
God never changeth;
Patient endurance
Attaineth to all things;
Who God possesseth
In nothing is wanting;
Alone God sufficeth.

TERESA OF AVILA
(TRANSLATED BY HENRY
WADSWORTH LONGFELLOW)

Modern Christian spirituality and theology don't help us much in this area either. The subject of patience has nearly disappeared from contemporary writing. As I began the research for this chapter, I looked for the word *patience* in my favorite dictionaries. Though patience has long been considered one of the major Christian virtues and was the subject of hundreds of treatises throughout Christian history, the word is conspicuously missing in current dictionaries of Christian spirituality and theology. It isn't even listed as a subject in many contemporary collections of prayers; when it is listed, there are only a couple of references. Perhaps it isn't surprising that we struggle with the concept of patience today; even the scholars shy away from the subject.[6]

I won't go into the details of the long history of Christian discourse on the subject here, but some common perceptions and misperceptions might be worth

Hearing with the Heart

considering. Patience has a bad name today. In part, that may be because we associate it with suffering and deprivation. We think that patience means smiling perfectly, no matter what is done to us, even if we are seething inside. But that view of patience allows great evil to exist in the world. In this view of patience, the poverty-stricken and abused are told to smile and be glad for what they have when this understanding of patience is accepted. In fact, patient people don't accept abuse and poverty at all; they work—sometimes very impatiently—to combat it. When we are trying to discern God's will for our lives or for the world around us, we're not asked to just sit around, be miserable, and smile happily all the while. We're not called to accept the world as it is and just assume that whatever happens is God's will. Like the man in the joke at the beginning of the chapter, we're allowed to express our frustration with God. We get to be angry, annoyed, frustrated, and even impatient. Patience, in this context, means that we stay engaged with God, that we keep listening and arguing if need be, that we not leave God out of the process and try to take charge ourselves. Patience means being like Job.

Job has the reputation of being a patient man. We compliment another's long-suffering endurance of difficulty by saying that he has "the patience of Job." But if patience equals quiet and gracious waiting and endurance, despite the circumstances, Job doesn't qualify. He did a lot of arguing, cursing, fussing, and fuming before he got there. He wanted to know what he did to deserve the loss of everything he held dear; in fact, he wanted a trial so he could be proven innocent. At other times, he just asked to die. Job threatened God at moments: "Remember that my life is a breath; / my eye will never again see good. / The eye that beholds me will see me no more; / while your eyes are upon me, I shall be gone" (Job 7:7–8). Job even accuses God of immorality: "The earth is given into the hand of the wicked; / he covers the eyes of its judges— / if it is not he, who then is it?" (Job 9:24). And Job certainly wasn't quiet and long-suffering with his three unhelpful friends—the ones who had all the answers, whose comfort was pretty cold. Job's words are hardly those of a patient man, at least not as we usually think of patience.

Lord, give me patience in tribulation and grace in everything to conform my will to thine.

THOMAS MORE

Be still before the LORD, and wait patiently for him.

PSALM 37:7

But patience is more than just enduring what comes without complaining. The *Oxford English Dictionary* also defines *patience* as "constancy in labor, exertion, or effort." And Job is nothing if not constant in his effort—and outright demand—to understand. So should we be in the process of discernment. As long as God is a partner in the conversation, we can fuss and fume, we can demand to know what God's will is, we can express our frustration when the answers aren't instantly forthcoming. To pretend that we're not angry, irritated, impatient, or tired of waiting doesn't fool God anyway. The key, as the nineteenth-century German poet Rainer Maria Rilke writes, is to keep loving the questions. In his famous book *Letters to a Young Poet,* Rilke gives this advice to a young would-be poet:

Be patient toward all that is unsolved in your heart and try to love the *questions themselves* like locked rooms and like books that are written in a very foreign language. Do not now seek the answers, which cannot be

Hearing with the Heart

given you because you would not be able to live them. And the point is, to live everything. *Live* the questions now. Perhaps you will then gradually, without noticing it, live along some distant day into the answer.[7]

As long as we keep listening for God rather than dismissing the question of God's will and making decisions without God, as long as we keep living the questions, we're being patient like Job.

Job never got really clear answers to his questions, not ones that make perfect sense to us anyway. But he did seem to find some peace of mind in his exchange with God. In Archibald MacLeish's contemporary play *J.B.,* based on the story of Job, the story ends with Job's wife, Sarah, expressing the hope and confidence that God's will would become clear at some point. "Blow on the coal of the heart. / The candles in churches are out. / The lights have gone out in the sky. / Blow on the coal of the heart / And we'll see by and by."[8] There will be times in our discernment when the answers are clear and times when the only answer seems to be silence, but patience in the process means that we stay in conversation with God, answers or no, and remain hopeful and confident that we'll see by and by.

THE ACTIVE HEART

The kind of patience we've been exploring is actually the key to the next step in the process: action. "Patience is the catalyst without which we shall not engage in productive activity," writes David Harned. "There is a strict correlation between the decline of patience and the loss of the capacity for action; they flourish together and wither in isolation."[9]

The story "Three Little Pigs" is the perfect example of what happens when action and patience aren't mixed in the right proportions. The three pigs all leave home at the same time, presumably to seek new adult lives. How they will live and what they will value is up to them now. The first little pig meets someone on the road with a cart full of straw and instantly decides to buy it and build a house. The farmer warns him that a house of straw isn't very sturdy, but the first pig dismisses the farmer's concern. Apparently, he has no time to listen to others or consider their advice; he is impatient to begin his new life. So he builds the house, the wolf comes along and blows it down, and the impatient pig is the wolf's dinner that night. The same thing happens to the second pig, who builds a house of sticks, despite advice to the contrary. He, too, becomes dinner for the wolf.

The third little pig is a bit smarter. On the advice of the bricklayer, he builds a house of bricks—a project that takes considerably more time than building

> *Christ has no body now on earth but yours;*
> *yours are the only hands with which he can do his work,*
> *yours are the only feet with which he can go about the world.*
> *Yours are the only eyes through which his compassion can shine forth upon*
> *a troubled world.*
> *Christ has no body now on earth but yours.*
>
> TERESA OF AVILA

houses of straw or sticks. His patience and his willingness to consider the opinions of others in the process pay off. His house is strong and sturdy, a safe refuge. Because this pig is also smarter than the first two, he manages to escape the wolf's trickery and presumably lives happily ever after. Unlike the other two pigs, he balances patience with right action.

The story of the pigs isn't a particularly religious one; we don't have any indication that God or discernment plays any particular part in the narrative. The point of the story is simply that the last little pig got to live. But for us, patience and action are balanced for a reason, and that reason is God. "A belief that God acts with purpose in this world must lead to attempts, however feeble, to discern how my own actions might be attuned to God's one action," concludes William Barry. "These attempts to discern must lead to action, otherwise I will be acting with 'bad faith.'"[10] Acting, of course, isn't always easy. What would you have said to Jesus if he had told you to sell everything you had, give the money to the poor, and follow him? (Mark 10:21). Fortunately for us, we're not usually invited to such drastic action.

Another childhood story, Kenneth Grahame's *Wind in the Willows,* illustrates an attempt to discern and act on God's will, even when the way isn't entirely clear, which is most of the time. In particular, the chapter titled "The Piper at the Gates of Dawn" speaks clearly about action that comes from and leads to the heart. If you don't know Grahame's book, it was published in England in 1908 and has been a classic in children's libraries ever since. The book centers around the lives of four animals who act remarkably like us, with all our foibles and successes.

In this particular chapter, Little Portly, the baby otter, is missing. Portly likes to wander, so it isn't unusual for him to be gone awhile, but he has been gone much too long now, and Portly's parents are worried sick. Rat and Mole are discussing this late at night, worried not only for Portly but for Portly's father, who is keeping watch at one of Portly's favorite spots. Their hearts are full of compassion and concern: Rat and Mole "were silent for a time, both thinking of the same thing—the lonely, heart-sore animal, crouched by the ford, watching and waiting, the long night through."[11] They discuss going to bed, as the hour is quite late, but neither of them moves. Finally, they decide that they simply must do something to help.

> "Rat," said the Mole, "I simply can't go and turn in, and go to sleep, and *do* nothing, even though there doesn't seem to be anything to be done. We'll get the boat out, and paddle upstream. The moon will be up in an hour or so, and then we will search as well as we can—anyhow, it will be better than going to bed and doing *nothing*."[12]

This is action that comes from patience. Everyone has waited a reasonable amount of time for Portly to come home. They've looked for him in all the usual spots, but to no avail. It is also action that comes from the heart. Compassion calls Rat and Mole to do what they can, both for Portly's sake and for his family's. Neither Rat nor Mole knows where Portly is; they don't have a vision or dream that reveals his whereabouts, but they know they are called to try to so *something*. So they set out in their boat, in the dark. They pick a direction—upstream—and they look for Portly in the dark, knowing that their chances of finding him in the night are slim.

This is so often the way we begin to take action on what we've discerned as well. Having heard with the heart, we know we are called to action, but what kind of action isn't always clear. I remember going on an interview for a job I was sure I wouldn't take. I'd been talking with the employer for months but didn't sense any call to take the position. It meant a major move, and I was pretty happy living where I was. I was so sure I wasn't called to that position that I'd bought theater tickets for the upcoming seasons without any concern. But in the middle of the interview, I discovered a strong sense of calling to the position. I just knew that I was supposed to be a part of that team. I remember getting to the airport to go home and calling a friend to express my surprise that I was, apparently, going to be moving. I had no idea how and when that would happen or what it would mean in my life, but I knew I was going along for the ride, whatever that turned out to be. Discernment can be like that. We get an inkling about what is coming—an invitation to move in some direction. And we begin to move, not really knowing what the implications of that will be. We only know that we have to do something, that it will be better than doing nothing.

Give us grace, O God, to dare to do the deed which we well know cries to be done.

W.E.B. DU BOIS

O Lord, give us grace not only to be hearers of the word, but also doers of the same.

THOMAS BACON

But back to Rat and Mole. They set out in their boat to search for Portly, and the traveling is difficult. In the middle of the stream they find a "clear, narrow track," the only thing they can follow in the dark. Even that is fraught with shadows that look like objects to avoid, so the going is tough. But in the quiet of the night, they also hear sounds that usually get drowned out in the noisiness of the daylight hours. Gurgling water, the chatter and rustling of animals and plants provide a pleasant backdrop to their difficult journey. Finally, the moon rises and the "mystery and terror" of their journey are transformed into beauty and radiance. Rat and Mole's "old haunts greeted them again in other raiment, as if they had slipped away and put on this pure new apparel and come quietly back, smiling as they shyly waited to see if they would be recognized again under it."[13] Action that was begun tentatively, in the dark, is transformed at some point. Light is provided—in this case, the relatively dim light of the moon. But even that amount of light provides comfort; it brings about transformation and pulls them forward.

Rat and Mole search by moonlight for hours, exploring the banks of the river, moving slowly upstream. The moonlight "serene and detached in a cloudless sky, did what she could, though so far off, to help them in their quest; till her hour came and she sank earthwards reluctantly, and left them, and mystery once more held field and river."[14] Everyone and everything is doing their best to help, but Portly is not to be found throughout the long night. But Rat and Mole are patient. Knowing that their action is right—that they must try to help find the baby otter—they persist. We, too, will probably find the way unclear at times, even when we are convinced that we are on the right track.

As Rat and Mole continue on, the sun begins to appear on the horizon, and again the world takes on a new look—a much clearer one this time. Suddenly, Rat comes to full attention; he has heard a sound—a beautiful, strange, and new sound—and he is desperate to hear it again.

"Now it passes on and I begin to lose it [the sound]," he said presently. "O Mole! the beauty of it! The merry bubble and joy, the thin, clear, happy call of the distant piping! Such music I never dreamed of, and the call in it is stronger even than the music is sweet! Row on, Mole, row! For the music and the call must be for us."

Mole doesn't hear the sound at all, but he continues to row, while the rapt Rat, in his ecstasy, urges them onward. That is sometimes our experience of action as well. We hear the call; we know what we are supposed to do, even when those around don't yet hear what we hear. But a few moments later, Mole begins to hear the call as well.

> Breathless and transfixed the Mole stopped rowing, as the liquid run of that glad piping broke on him like a wave, caught him up, and possessed him utterly. . . . For a space they hung there . . . then the clear imperious summons that marched hand-in-hand with the intoxicating melody imposed its will on Mole, and mechanically he bent to his oars again. . . . They felt a consciousness that they were nearing the end, whatever it might be, that surely awaited their expedition.[15]

That is our experience, too, when the action we take is right action. We may begin in darkness, but if the action is, indeed, the one that God calls us to, light begins to dawn and we find our way. Rat and Mole continue to follow the music they hear and come to a small island in the stream that they know—in their hearts—is the source of what calls them. "'This is the place of my song-dream, the place the music played to me,' whispered Rat, as if in a trance. 'Here, in this holy place, here if anywhere, surely we shall find Him!' "[16] The light grows stronger and stronger as Rat and Mole make their way to a clearing, the source of the call. There they are struck by awe, an "awe that turned [Mole's] muscles to water. . . . It was an awe that smote and held him and, without seeing, he knew it could only mean that some august Presence was very, very near."[17] A presence does appear to Rat and Mole. They look "into the very eyes of the Friend and Helper," and Portly is sleeping at the feet of that Presence. The light grows brighter and brighter and finally hits them full in the face, and the Presence disappears, leaving Portly to wake up and discover his friends. After a cheerful reunion with the baby otter, Rat and Mole take Portly home to his worried family.

> *The word is very near to you; it is in your mouth and in your heart for you to observe.*
>
> DEUTERONOMY 30:14

This is, of course, a story, and our own experience of right action as a result of discerning God's call is unlikely to be quite as dramatic as this. Still, this is the story of what it is like to hear and respond to God's call for us. We can be called to do something as basic as what Rat and Mole did—to find a lost young one. The proper action, in response to our patient discernment, may be teaching a nursery school class or becoming a librarian. Maybe we're called to volunteer our talents, like a friend of mine, an editor, who spent a week writing media releases and talking to the press on behalf of the Red Cross after the terrorist attacks on the World Trade Center towers in 2001.

I got a very pointed lesson about action once at a conference of spiritual directors where I was speaking. At the dinner table, a woman asked me if I did my spiritual direction through my books or if I met with people one-on-one. I quickly responded that I wasn't a spiritual director at all. But my own spiritual director, sitting next to me, quickly responded, "Through her books." We tend to think of ordinary actions as inconsequential, beneath God's radar. But God needs all kind of co-creators in this world, including the ones who will give everything they have to the poor and those who can teach a nursery school class with grace and love.

We begin the journey tentatively in darkness—partial or complete. We take classes to learn what we need to know or talk to others about our choices and learn more about what we'll need for the journey. We do something rather than nothing. As William Barry so pointedly states, "'Religious beliefs' that do not issue in action in accordance with them are simply thoughts about the world, not beliefs."[18] And if the action is a right one, light begins to dawn. Things and people around us begin to look different. When we persevere and continue to follow the call we've heard with our heart, the light grows, and somewhere along the way, we find ourselves exactly where we are supposed to be, doing just what God has called us to do. So be it, and amen.

Chapter Ten

EPILOGUE

There is no guarantee that God will act in a certain way toward someone trying to live a good life. One plants one's feet firmly in midair and marches on in faith, hope, and trust. The only verification we get is continued peace and joy on the journey.[1]

WILLIAM A. BARRY

Planting your feet firmly in midair, as William Barry writes in the epigraph, and moving forward with hopefulness hardly seems like an appropriate reward for all the work of discernment. Upon arriving at the "right answer" about the direction of my life, I'd rather something more definite happened. I'd like something really clear, like a contestant on a game show gets, where the correct and final answer is rewarded with flashing lights, loud noises, a smiling host, and cheers and claps from the audience. At the very least, I would like some sage figure to nod her head at me, smiling knowingly. I definitely don't want to be like the Desert Father whom others accused of sleeping with his female servant rather than being chaste, as they believed God desired of them. On his deathbed, he instructed the others to plant a stick on his grave. If it bore fruit, they would know he had been pure. It bore fruit, of course, but that's a pretty tough way to prove that you followed God's desires for you.

But like it or not, no one awards gold stars for correct discernment. We have to just plant our feet firmly in midair in hope that we have discerned well. Trappist monk and writer Thomas Merton expressed what it is like to move forward at this stage, even in the midst of uncertainty, in a poem:

O Lord God,
I have no idea where I am going,
I do not see the road ahead of me,
I cannot know for certain where it will end.
Nor do I really know myself,
and the fact that I think
I am following your will
does not mean that I am actually doing so.
But I believe
that the desire to please you does in fact please you,
and I hope I have that desire
in all that I am doing.

I hope that I will never do anything
apart from that desire to please you.
And I know that if I do this
you will lead me by the right road,
though I may know nothing about it.
Therefore I will trust you always
though I may seem to be lost
and in the shadow of death.
I will not fear,
for you are ever with me,
and you will never leave me
to make my journey alone.[2]

THOMAS MERTON

His poem points out, so rightly, that we cannot know if we are actually following God's intention for us and if we are truly pleasing God. But—and it is a big "but"—we have to believe that our desire and our efforts to live as God calls us to live do, in fact, please God. And just as we know when what we are doing and how we are living pleases friends and family, there are signs that can help us feel at least some confidence that our lives please God as well. None of these signs can be used as a single litmus test of our discernment. But the more of them that apply to what we have discerned, the more confident we can feel that we are, indeed, listening well with our hearts and following God.

THE HEART'S DESIRES FULFILLED

A true call usually comes with the sense that your heart's deepest desires are being fulfilled. The Quakers call it a *leading*. "A true leading," writes Charlotte Fardelmann, "touches a deep level in oneself. It resonates on the level with our deepest desires. When we talk about it to others, we show excitement."[3] These heart's desires aren't the ones that tell us we want a new black sweater this winter but ones that live deep within us and have been there for a long time. In *Nudged by the Spirit,* Fardelmann shares stories of Quakers and their experiences of discernment. One of the stories is about a British woman who was raised in Thailand, where she was exposed to a wide variety of people, faiths, and beliefs. When she was five, her family moved back to England, where she was exposed to the Anglican Church; there she heard others denigrate religious traditions outside of Anglicanism. The seed of ecumenism—an interest in understanding and being with people of many faith perspectives—was planted in her from her youngest days and never quite left her.

She eventually joined the Society of Friends, and when the World Council of Churches was to come to Vancouver for their 1983 General Assembly, she served on the host program committee. One thing led to another, and finally she was invited to represent the Canadian Yearly Meeting of Friends on the World Council itself. Of that invitation she says, "I have found this many times in my life: God gets me to a place where he needs me to be by whatever means he can get me there, and then I find out when I am there why I am really there."[4]

Many of us could say that same thing about that moment or time when we discovered, deep in our hearts, that we finally sensed what God was inviting us to do or be. There is often a feeling, particularly as we look backward, that the seed was there all along. Often, though not always, what we sense we are being called to is either consistent with what we've identified as our gifts or a natural evolution of the path we've been on, even if the path has been an unconscious one. When the invitation is finally recognized and accepted, there is the sense that our own little mustard seed can now sprout into a wonderful tree or that we can stop swimming upstream.

That friend I mentioned in Chapter Two who gave up his prestigious and lucrative job to go into business for himself is working lots of hours still, probably just as many as he did when he worked for a corporation. But he's enjoying himself much more. He's got more customers than he can actually manage at any given time, but they're willing to wait for his services, because he's wonderful at helping his clients pursue their own dreams and make them into reality. Working for himself, he's no longer hindered from doing his own best by corporate goals, procedures, and quotas. And he's just plain happier.

Another friend of mine, a pastor I'll call Carol, decided not to become the pastor of a church, largely on her sense that the particular place was not right for her. She'd applied for the position because it was located in a city where she'd lived much of her life—a place she loved and wanted to return to. Though she wasn't unhappy with her current church, she felt she simply had to explore the possibility of returning to a place that was home for her. After spending months in conversation with the selection committee, she went to visit for the weekend and discovered, much to her surprise, that the church itself and the people simply didn't call to her. They weren't her heart's desire, and she wasn't theirs. She withdrew from the process, and the committee selected their new pastor very soon after that—a further sign to Carol that she'd been right to pay attention to her sense that the call wasn't there.

O God, unto whom all hearts are open, all desires known, and from whom no secrets are hid, cleanse the thoughts of our hearts by the inspiration of thy Holy Spirit, that we may perfectly love thee and worthily magnify thy Holy Name, through Christ our Lord. Amen.

"THE COLLECT FOR PURITY," THE BOOK OF COMMON PRAYER

The heart's desire is not a sure signal of a true sense of God's desires for us. Nothing is simple in discernment! Jonah, for instance, never desired to go to Ninevah when God called him there, and he never developed any affection for the call, so far as we know. Maybe it served some purpose in Jonah's life later on, but in the short snapshot of his life that appears in the Bible, we find a pretty cranky and frustrated Jonah who finds little value in this particular call.

Moses wasn't too excited by what God said to him from the burning bush either, though I wonder if God's desire to have Moses free his people didn't fulfill Moses' heart's desire after all. Imagine how Moses must have felt, living as an Egyptian all of his young years, watching his own people being beaten and brutalized. It made him angry enough to kill an Egyptian overseer one day—a deed that forced him out of Egypt. Maybe Moses' heart's desire really was to free his people, and God gave him the way to do it.

Hearing with the Heart

The sense of a call that fulfills your deepest desire is important, though it cannot be trusted in and of itself. What is evil in this world can use the heart's desire to call you forward as well. God's name has been invoked many times when exterminating races, enslaving people, and committing violence against people, animals, and the earth. As with all other tests of the clarity of our discernments, this sense of rightness must exist along with many of the other elements described in this chapter. But if you feel that what you are being called to do or to be is a "homecoming" of sorts, if it feels right deep in your heart, you have at least one clue that your desire may be in accord with God's.

THE NEEDS OF THE WORLD

A true call not only fulfills your own heart's desires but serves others as well. We are not called to act in ways that are senseless, futile, or irrational for ourselves or for others. Our poor monk, Hero, for instance, might have questioned his sense of God's desire that he jump down a well; it was an action that led only to Hero's own ego satisfaction, with no redeeming value for anyone else or anything around him. If the call you are sensing includes nothing of benefit for the world around you, chances are you are not hearing clearly.

As with the first test of your call—the heart's desires—the fact that you believe you are being called to serve others does not guarantee that you've discerned clearly. I took a job once because I thought I could fix everything that was wrong with the organization I was joining. I believed I could improve the quality of the organization and the lives of the people who worked there. I turned out to be quite wrong. I fixed little or nothing during my time there and experienced a huge amount of frustration in the process. Reflecting back on that time, I realize that I took the job out of my own ego needs—a desire that everyone see what an amazing manager I was—instead of out of any sense of having a call. I learned the hard way that it isn't all that difficult to fool ourselves about what we believe God is asking us to do, especially when we believe that what we think we are called to seems noble in some way.

Brother Roger, the founder of the French Taizé religious community, did a better job of discerning clearly than I did when I took the wrong job. In 1940, he was twenty-five years old and living in Switzerland—a place of relative peace during World War II. Disturbed by the war around him, he was filled with the desire to begin a monastic community dedicated to reconciliation. He moved to France, to a small house in the village of Taizé, a town very close to the demarcation line that cut France in two at that time. He lived there for two years, taking Jews and other political refugees into hiding. After having his house searched many times by the Germans, he was forced to flee France but came back in 1944 and began his monastic community in earnest. Over the years, Taizé has become a place of true reconciliation—an ecumenical community rather than just a Catholic one. And it has become a place where people, particularly youth, of all

Forth in thy name, O Lord I go
My daily labour to pursue:
Thee, only thee, resolved to know,
In all I think, or speak, or do.
The task thy wisdom hath assign'd
O let me cheerfully fulfill:
In all my works thy presence find,
And prove thy good and perfect Will.

CHARLES WESLEY

denominations and perspectives come to pray and be with others from around the world. Today, Taizé attracts thousands of visitors a week.

Your story doesn't need to be as dramatic as Brother Roger's; in all likelihood it won't be. But the same principle applies to your own vocational decisions and even the everyday discernments you make. Does your choice of volunteer work or the charities to which you choose to give meet the needs of others in a way that seems in accord with God's desires? Do you interact with others in a way that builds up people, and animals, and the earth itself or tears them down? Even a discernment to recycle your garbage may come from a desire to help meet the needs of our planet by using resources wisely so that there is plenty to go around for everyone.

TESTING OUR TRUE MOTIVES

"A healthy skepticism of our own motives is a sign of spiritual maturity," writes Suzanne Farnham and her colleagues in *Listening Hearts*.[5] We've looked at many stories—old and new—where people have managed to fool themselves about what God asks of them throughout this book. We're human beings, and human beings are fallible. But as we mature spiritually, it becomes easier to look at our own foibles with both a knowing eye and some gentleness of spirit. Watching for the ways in which we fool ourselves and avoiding the traps is like disciplining a child; it can be done with firmness and kindness at the same time.

One of the dangers to watch for is a desire for change that involves running away from problems or frustrations rather than moving toward a true calling.

Ignatius of Loyola and many others in the field of discernment caution against making major moves when we are very unhappy, when we are experiencing "desolation" or distress. During these times, it is all too easy to move from the proverbial frying pan into the fire. Our motives for wanting a change when we are caught in a situation we find frustrating or unsatisfying need to be questioned carefully and usually with the assistance of others. That doesn't mean that we never move toward a new sense of call when we are unhappy with our lives as they exist, but it is vitally important to truly determine that we are moving toward something rather than simply trying to get away from something we dislike.

We also have to guard against jumping from place to place or making ever-new decisions because we are bored or because we are finding difficulties where we are. Moving to a new geographical location, a new job, a new church, and so on are commonplace today, and although that is sometimes exciting, we have given up a great deal by being essentially rootless. We keep seeking God's call over the next hill, but the reality is that if we don't find God where we are, we are unlikely to find God over the next hill either. The Desert Fathers tell the story of a brother who came to ask the advice of Abba Moses. Moses' response was sim-

O God, from whom to be turned is to fall, to whom to be turned is to rise, and in whom to stand is to abide for ever: grant us in all our duties your help, in all our perplexities your guidance, in all our dangers your protection, and in all our sorrows your peace.

AUGUSTINE OF HIPPO

Hearing with the Heart

ple: "Go sit in your cell, and your cell will teach you everything."[6] No doubt this brother had journeyed many miles to gather Abba Moses' advice, and we sometimes do the same in our own lives, when the answer is actually to stay put and experience the richness of being grounded in our own backyard.

Perhaps the opposite of our desire to jump from place to place or job to job is the fear of change. I know someone who grew up in the Great Depression of the 1930s in America, and he thinks it is flighty to leave a job after only ten years. Change, in general, is difficult for him. Some of that is probably generational—a set of values his generation holds dear. But part is also that he feels the uncertainty he felt during his childhood years in the Depression. Unfortunately, responding to God's desires for us often brings anxiety with it. Moses wasn't exactly thrilled when God, speaking from the burning bush, asked him to free the Hebrews enslaved in Egypt. Even Christ asked that the cup of crucifixion be taken from him, if it be God's will. Calls and the changes that come with them can produce anxiety sometimes. We may be invited to give up financial comfort and status or to move to a whole new place. But calls also bring great joy. If you sense that God's call to you involves only sacrifice and no joy, then you are probably mistaken about what God is asking of you.

> *Teach me, my God and King,*
> *In all things thee to see,*
> *And what I do in anything,*
> *To do it as for thee.*
>
> GEORGE HERBERT

All of these feelings—a desire for change or to avoid it; anxiety, boredom, or sadness—are difficult to navigate during discernment, particularly when the decision feels like a major one for your life. We don't really know what our heart is feeling sometimes or which way to turn. That's why friends, spiritual advisers, and communities are so important to the process. We need people to talk to during these difficult times, and we need to hear their confirmation—or lack thereof—for the path we think God calls us to take.

CONFIRMATION OVER AND OVER AGAIN

In an episode of *Star Trek: The Next Generation,* a popular television show that takes place in space, a starship, the *Enterprise,* was stuck in a time loop of some sort. Over and over, the people on the ship repeated a series of events, and as they did so, more and more started to have a sense of déjà vu. Finally, after performing the same events for many days (seventeen of them, as it turned out), they guessed what was happening to them and left themselves a clue—the number 3—that allowed them to escape the time loop and get on their way. Everywhere the ship's crew looked, on the last repetition of the cycle they found the number 3. Sometimes discernment is like that. It seems as if every time we turn around, someone else says or does something, or we feel a desire within ourselves, or perhaps we have a string of "coincidences" that confirms that a particular path is the one in accord with God's desires for us. Think of it as a mosquito buzzing around your ear; no matter how many times you swat it away, it keeps coming back.

"I did not mean for all of this to happen to me. Or any of it, for that matter," writes Robert Benson, in his spiritual autobiography, *Living Prayer.* Benson goes on to describe a simple series of events—none of them terribly major or important—that brought him to a deeper relationship with God. It began with a desire to have a more formal prayer life—a notion that seemed to come out of the blue. Then his father gave him a daily devotional book. He didn't open the book for years, but on the day he did open it, he looked out his window, across the fields, and at the steeple of a small church that friends of his attended, and something opened up in him. At the time, he was an editor of other people's books and a ghost writer—work he compared to doing other people's laundry. Looking at the church across the field that morning, he decided to call the pastor and ask if he might write at the church. Much to his surprise, the pastor said yes, and so began a time of praying and writing in the church building. These simple events—a deep desire that came "from nowhere," the gift of a book, seeing the church from his window, which he'd seen hundreds of times before, and a moment of transcendence one day while playing basketball—led Benson to respond to his sense that God was calling him to write his own words rather than edit those of others. All of those events Benson could simply have ignored; they didn't have to be filled with any meaning in particular. But they were not coincidences or events without meaning, and it was Benson's ability to pay attention to God calling him that allowed him to notice that something was happening and to hear with his heart.

> Lord, be a bright flame before me,
> be a guiding star above me,
> be a smooth path below me,
> be a kindly shepherd behind me,
> today and for evermore. Amen.
>
> COLUMBIA

These kinds of events occur in all of our lives. They're like clues in a mystery novel. Somebody says something that turns out to be very important later on. You're given or come across an item that speaks to you, that carries significance somehow. A thought keeps crossing your mind over days, weeks, months—even years. Or a dream comes to you repeatedly. "Circumstance and coincidence may cause us to be in the right place at the right time to do God's work in a specific way," writes Suzanne Farnham in *Listening Hearts*. "This may be a sign that God is calling us."[7] All of these may be confirmations that you've truly identified God's desires for you.

THE TEST OF SCRIPTURE

Books on discernment routinely tell us that when we believe we have discerned God's wishes for us, we should test that discernment against what is written in the Bible. Although I think that's generally true, it is also one of the most difficult ways of testing our call. With which part of scripture should our call be consistent? There are so many violent stories and suggestions in the Bible—stories of wars and incredible violence leveled against people. The psalms alone are filled with tremendous anger and with requests that God kill the enemies and care only for the righteous. Thomas Jefferson dealt with these very difficult narratives by "creating" his own version of the Bible—the Jefferson Bible; he simply cut the difficult stories out of his Bible, leaving only more pleasant stories and passages. Others have done much the same with the gospels. But that doesn't solve the problem, because there are times when we are actually called to righteous anger, to defend the oppressed, to channel our anger or frustration in a way that builds the world up.

Others have dealt with the violence in the Hebrew scriptures by asserting that discernment should be tested against the stories of the life of Jesus in the New

Testament. Although that has some merit, it leaves us without the rich stories of Moses, Jonah, Ruth, the prophets, and others—a tremendous loss when we are looking to scripture to help illuminate our path or confirm that we're hearing rightly. Still other writers claim, correctly, that we have to look at scripture with the context of the writer's time and agenda in mind. True again, but you still have the problem of wondering which piece of scripture and context you should be considering. "Many people hold that scripture provides the guidelines for right action," writes Gerald May, "and in a large sense it does. It gives general principles, but scripture is a living, loving word, so it more often deepens my questions about specific situations than gives me answers."[8]

Perhaps the most helpful suggestion I can make to you is that the more grounded you are in scripture, the more time you've spent reading and studying it, the more you will develop an overall sense of God's desires for you and the world around you. And the more you can do that within a community that is also grounded in scripture, the more accurate your understanding of God's will is likely to be. Studying with those who are scholars of scripture, listening to the interpretations and thoughts of others about particular books of the Bible or particular passages, and reflecting on the application of those stories is not only thought provoking and enriching but it opens your heart further. It may even cast significant light on a particular decision you are trying to make or help you explore your confusion about a path. This kind of study and reflection on the Bible provides you with a good grounding for testing the call you think you are hearing from God, not in any way that is hard and fast but for recognizing that, in an overall sense, the path you feel you are being asked to walk is consistent with God's will as understood through scripture. Scripture, in short, is a clue for testing the call you discern, but it isn't a litmus test that proves you got the right answer.

BODY CONFIRMATION

I remember one time in my life when I was trying to discern if God was inviting me to take a new step. After struggling with the decision for a couple of months, I decided to move forward, though I felt some hesitancy about the decision. "Are you feeling excited about your choice?" a friend asked me, when I told him what I was planning to do. I answered that I was feeling mostly a sense of anxiety and of some loss about what I was leaving behind but that I was sure excitement would come after I dealt with those feelings. But as I listened to myself, I realized that I was rationalizing—that I had not discerned well after all. My choice was keeping me awake nights, as I worried about the consequences of my decision. I felt no excitement, no sense of peace in my body. I was rushing my decision, trying to get away from something that troubled me, picking the first available path rather than moving forward into a new call. The time was not right for the decision I had made.

> *Abide in me as I abide in you. Just as the branch cannot bear fruit by itself unless it abides in the vine, neither can you unless you abide in me.*
>
> JOHN 15:4

Our bodies and our emotions are usually good informants when it comes time to test the call we feel. A true discernment is usually accompanied by feelings of joy, peace, serenity, clarity, gratitude, or excitement, or feelings of surprise or humility about having been chosen for the particular call. You may even feel a sense of inadequacy, as Moses did when God sent him to free the Israelites. Moses resisted the call at first, telling God that he did not have the gift of words that he needed. But God sent Aaron along to help Moses. You may have the same kind of concerns about your gifts, but the anxiety about that should not overwhelm the joy you feel. You might also find yourself in tears once you understand your call, especially when it involves leaving someone or something behind as you move in your new direction. But if the call is true, the "negative" feelings—loss, anxiety—will not overwhelm the sense of joy, peace, or excitement. Or as Suzanne Farnham writes, "If the apparent good that comes to us is accompanied by vanity, anxiety, irritability, resentment, condemnation, or condescension, it may be a sign that we are not hearing God's call."[9]

If you worked through the material on paying attention to your body in Chapter Four earlier, you will also have a good barometer of your call as you notice what happens with your body. Does it respond positively, according to what you know about your own bodily responses? For me, positive responses include increased appetite, a strong sense of relaxation and energy, and an ability to sleep soundly. Negative or anxious responses include tightness in my stomach, insomnia, and pain in my back or neck. Your own body will probably respond differently than mine does, but awareness of how your body responds will help you to know if you are discerning well, with your heart, versus running away from something or making a decision that is based on something other than God's desires. Bodies rarely lie to us. I find my body to be one of the very best tests for knowing if I am on the right or wrong path.

CONFIRMED BY COMMUNITY

In many Christian denominations, an individual who senses a call to ordained ministry is given a committee of people whose task is to support the person while the discernment process continues. They ask questions meant to help bring about clarity. They pray with and for the person seeking his or her call. Sometimes they challenge what they are hearing from that person, and they offer encouragement when it is needed. Although these committees are not without their faults—we're human, after all—it is a shame that we all don't have this kind of community support as we try to discern the way ahead.

Guide me, O thou great Jehovah,
pilgrim through this barren land;
I am weak, but thou art mighty;
hold me with thy powerful hand;
bread of heaven, bread of heaven,
feed me now and evermore,
feed me now and evermore.

WILLIAM WILLIAMS

We all have some community, however, be that a church community, friends, family, spiritual director, soul friends, or whatever. And a good test of your discernment is your friends' and family's reactions to your sense of your own and God's desires for you. If there is widespread disagreement with your discernment among those you know—if there aren't folks sensing the same sense of direction you sense—it is quite possible you've discerned incorrectly. Imagine our monk, Hero, again, confronting others in his area about his "call" to jump into the well. There probably wasn't anyone around him who would have confirmed his choice.

What you may find is that some agree and some disagree about your sense of call. My friend who left corporate life, as I mentioned earlier, got resistance from

Hearing with the Heart

some in his business community. But those people closest to him—the people who knew him best and whom he trusted the most—were supportive of his discernment to go into business for himself. He had to choose to listen to those voices and dismiss others. And even though it is possible for all your friends, family, and spiritual community to be wrong about their assessment of your discernment, it is unlikely. If no one understands what you are sensing, it is time to wait and listen for a while longer.

THE FRUITS OF THE SPIRIT

Perhaps the best test of whether or not you have truly heard God's call with your heart is the test of time. Living in a way that is consistent with God's desires for you and the world around you results in what we commonly call the fruits of the Spirit—a phrase that comes from Galatians: "[T]he fruit of the Spirit is love, joy, peace, patience, kindness, generosity, faithfulness, gentleness, and self-control" (Galatians 5:22–23). When the long-term result of the action you take as a result of discerning with your heart are these fruits, then you have probably discerned clearly.

Some friends of mine, a pastor and his wife, moved to a new church a few years ago, based on a strong sense of call to that particular community. Their first year or two in the new parish were very difficult. Their house in the old community didn't sell for almost a year, causing quite a strain on the budget. And not long after arriving at the new church, they were embroiled in a church battle that had been brewing for many years, one that the pastor forced to the surface where people had to deal with it. The six months or so that they and the congregation spent working out that situation were as unpleasant a time as anyone could imagine, and the church nearly split in two. Some people did end up leaving the congregation, but the church resolved the problem and not only survived but flourished once this decades-old issue had been identified and repaired. The pastor and his wife had serious questions about their call amidst all the difficulties, but they persisted in their work with the congregation. In the end, the pastor turned out to have been just the right person to help the congregation expose the elephant in the middle of the room and banish it, which was essential to do if the congregation was to continue on and even grow. He and his wife came to realize that their sense of call had, indeed, been real. The results of their work there were the fruits of the Spirit. But it was very difficult to know that while they were in the midst of the anger and frustration of many in the congregation.

The fruit of the Spirit is love, joy, peace, patience, kindness, generosity, faithfulness, gentleness, and self-control.

GALATIANS 5:22–23

May I know Thee more clearly, love Thee more dearly, and follow Thee more nearly, day by day.

SAINT RICHARD OF CHICHESTER

True calls can be just like this one. We rarely know what is actually ahead of us when we accept them. If Moses had known how difficult his work was going to be, for instance, he might have said no to God, regardless of the consequences. Living as God desires is not like a Hollywood film, where "happily ever after" is the consequence of picking correctly. Neither is living God's way a call to difficulty and misery for the rest of our lives. We are all called to joy, peace, and whole-

Hearing with the Heart

ness; a discernment that results in nothing but anger and frustration is not a discernment from the heart. The results of following God's desires, in the long run, should be those listed in Galatians: love, joy, peace, patience, kindness, generosity, faithfulness, gentleness, and self-control. When they are not, you may have reason to question what you believe your heart has heard.

THE BENEDICTION

It is my deepest hope that this book helps you along the journey that leads us to the discerned life, one that has heard and responded with the heart. The trip is rarely easy, but the travel opens the heart to all kinds of new vistas, and the rewards are rich. I wish you a safe and exciting journey and leave you with a blessing from the ancient Celts:

> May the road rise to meet you;
> May the wind be always at your back;
> May the sun shine warm upon your face;
> May the rain fall soft upon your fields.
> And until we meet again,
> May the Lord hold you in the palm of his hand.

RESOURCE
A Prayer Service for Discernment

This service may be used individually or by a group that is working on discernment. Variations of the words to be used by groups are in parentheses. Groups may find it helpful to assign a leader for the Invitation to Prayer and the Collect for Guidance. Individuals in the group can be assigned to read the various scripture readings aloud to the rest of the group. Groups may also find it helpful to break into two groups and read antiphonally for the Psalm and the Prayers, with one group reading the first line, the other group reading the second line, and continuing to read back and forth to each other until the reading is complete. This allows everyone both to proclaim and to listen and is often a rewarding way to pray with others.

The structure of this service may be unfamiliar to you, and a few notes about the titles of the various parts may be helpful. The basic model is similar to ones used in Catholic, Anglican, and Lutheran worship services: a request for God's presence, readings from scripture, praise to God, and prayers. But some specific pieces may be new for you. A *canticle* is a song, often a song of praise. Canticles are often used to reinforce the message of the readings from scripture. A *collect* (the first syllable is emphasized instead of the second) is a form of prayer. Collects consist of one—usually quite long—sentence that focuses on a theme, often one that is consistent with the theme of the service.

The Invitation to Prayer

O Lord, open my (our) lips, and my (our) mouth(s) will declare your praise. (Psalm 51:15)

A Request for God's Presence and Guidance

Lord, teach me (us) to seek you, and reveal yourself to me (us) when I (we) seek you. For I (we) cannot seek you unless you first teach me (us), nor find you except you reveal yourself to me (us). Let me (us) seek you in longing, and long for you in seeking; let me (us) find you in love, and love you in finding, O Jesus Christ our Lord. Amen. (Ambrose of Milan)

The Greeting

I will bless the LORD at all times; God's praise shall continually be in my mouth. (Psalm 34:1)

The Psalm

How lovely is your dwelling place, O LORD of hosts!
My soul longs, indeed it faints for the courts of the LORD; my heart
and my flesh sing for joy to the living God.
Even the sparrow finds a home, and the swallow a nest for herself, where she
may lay her young, at your altars, O LORD of hosts, my King and my God.

Happy are those who live in your house, ever singing your praise. *Selah*

Happy are those whose strength is in you, in whose heart are the highways
to Zion.

As they go through the valley of Baca they make it a place of springs; the
early rain also covers it with pools.

They go from strength to strength; the God of gods will be seen in Zion.

O LORD God of hosts, hear my prayer; give ear, O God of Jacob! *Selah*

Behold our shield, O God; look on the face of your anointed.

For a day in your courts is better than a thousand elsewhere. I would rather
be a doorkeeper in the house of my God than live in the tents of wickedness.

For the LORD God is a sun and shield; he bestows favor and honor. No good
thing does the LORD withhold from those who walk uprightly.

O LORD of hosts, happy is everyone who trusts in you. (Psalm 84)

The Canticle

Seek the Lord while God wills to be found;
call upon God when he draws near.
Let the wicked forsake their ways
and the evil ones their thoughts;
And let them turn to the Lord, and God will have compassion,
and to our God, for God will richly pardon.
For my thoughts are not your thoughts,
nor your ways my ways, says the Lord.
For as the heavens are higher than the earth,

so are my ways higher than your ways,
and my thoughts than your thoughts.
For as rain and snow fall from the heavens,
and return not again, but water the earth,
Bringing forth life and giving growth,
seed for sowing and bread for eating,
So is my word that goes forth from my mouth;
it will not return to me empty;
But it will accomplish that which I have purposed,
and prosper in that for which I sent it.
(The Second Song of Isaiah, adapted from The Book of Common Prayer)

A period of silence may be observed here,
in order to meditate on the readings.

The Word

[Jesus said to them:] "I did not say these things to you from the beginning, because I was with you. But now I am going to him who sent me; yet none of you asks me, 'Where are you going?' But because I have said these things to you, sorrow has filled your hearts. Nevertheless I tell you the truth: it is to your advantage that I go away, for if I do not go away, the Advocate will not come to you; but if I go, I will send him to you. And when he comes, he will prove the world wrong about sin and righteousness and judgment. I still have many things to say to you, but you cannot bear them now. When the Spirit of truth comes, he will guide you into all the truth;

for he will not speak on his own, but will speak whatever he hears, and he will declare to you the things that are to come." (John 16:4–8, 12–13)

The Canticle

Seek the Lord while God wills to be found;
call upon God when he draws near.
Let the wicked forsake their ways
and the evil ones their thoughts;
And let them turn to the Lord, and God will have compassion,
and to our God, for God will richly pardon.
For my thoughts are not your thoughts,
nor your ways my ways, says the Lord.
For as the heavens are higher than the earth,
so are my ways higher than your ways,
and my thoughts than your thoughts.
For as rain and snow fall from the heavens,
and return not again, but water the earth,
Bringing forth life and giving growth,
seed for sowing and bread for eating,
So is my word that goes forth from my mouth;
it will not return to me empty;
But it will accomplish that which I have purposed, and prosper in that
for which I sent it.
(The Second Song of Isaiah, adapted from The Book of Common Prayer)

A period of silence may be observed here,
in order to meditate on the reading.

The Gloria

Glory to the Father, and to the Son, and to the Holy Spirit: as it was in the beginning, is now, and will be for ever. Amen.

(*Alternate*): Glory be to the Creator, and to the Christ, and to the Holy Spirit: as it was in the beginning, is now, and will be for ever. Amen.

The Prayers

If this service is being used by a group, half the group can read the first line, the other half the second line, and so on. Or a leader can read the first line, the group the second line, and so on.

> Show us your mercy, O Lord;
> And grant us your salvation.
> Clothe your ministers with righteousness;
> Let your people sing with joy.
> Give peace, O Lord, in all the world;
> For only in you can we live in safety.
> Lord, keep this nation under your care;

And guide us in the way of justice and truth.
Let your way be known upon earth;
Your saving health among all nations.
Let not the needy, O Lord, be forgotten;
Nor the hope of the poor be taken away.
Create in us clean hearts, O God;
And sustain us with your Holy Spirit.

Private prayers and petitions
may be offered here.

The Lord's Prayer

Our Father (Creating God) in heaven,
hallowed be your Name,
your kingdom come,
your will be done,
on earth as in heaven.
Give us today our daily bread.
Forgive us our sins
as we forgive those who sin against us.
Save us from the time of trial,
and deliver us from evil.
For the kingdom, the power, and the glory are yours, now and for ever. Amen.

Collect for Guidance

Gracious and loving God, in you we live and move and have our being: We humbly pray you so to guide us and govern us by your Holy Spirit, that in all the cares and occupations of our life we may not forget you, but may remember that we are ever walking in your sight; through Jesus Christ our Lord. Amen.

Concluding Prayer

Gracious God, you have promised that you will guide us continually, satisfy our needs in parched places, and make our bones strong. You promised that we will be like a watered garden, like a spring of water, whose waters never fail. Glory to you, whose power, working in us, can do infinitely more than we can ask or imagine: Glory to you from generation to generation, and in Christ Jesus for ever and ever. Amen.

NOTES

Introduction

1 Anthony De Mello, *The Song of the Bird* (New York: Doubleday, 1982), pp. 3–4.

Chapter One

1 Quoted in Rueben P. Job, comp., *A Guide to Spiritual Discernment* (Nashville, Tenn.: Upper Room Books, 1996), p. 29

2 Paul J. Achtemeier, ed., *HarperCollins Dictionary,* rev. ed. (New York: HarperCollins, 1996), p. 408.

3 Helen Waddell, trans., *The Desert Fathers* (New York: Vintage Books, 1998), p. 68.

4 Marjorie Hewitt Suchocki, *In God's Presence: Theological Reflections on Prayer* (St. Louis: Chalice Press, 1996), p. 4.

5 L. William Countryman and M. R. Ritley, *Gifted by Otherness: Gay and Lesbian Christians in the Church* (Harrisburg, Pa.: Morehouse, 2001), p. 21.

6 Colm Luibheid, trans., *John Cassian: Conferences* (Mahwah, N.J.: Paulist Press, 1985), p. 61.

7 Robert Benson, *Between the Dreaming and the Coming True* (New York: Tarcher, 2001), pp. 60–61.

8 Antoine de Saint-Exupéry, *The Little Prince* (Orlando, Fla.: Harcourt Brace, 1934).

9 Luibheid, *John Cassian,* pp. 64–65.

10 John Bunyan, *The Pilgrim's Progress* (New York: New American Library, n.d.).

11 William A. Barry, *Paying Attention to God: Discernment in Prayer* (Notre Dame, Ind.: Ave Maria Press, 1990), p. 60.

Chapter Two

1 Anne Lamott, *Traveling Mercies: Some Thoughts on Faith* (New York: Pantheon Books, 1999), p. 250.

2 Roberta C. Bondi, *Memories of God: Theological Reflections on a Life* (Nashville, Tenn.: Abingdon Press, 1995), p. 25.

3 Wendy M. Wright, "Passing Angels: The Arts of Spiritual Discernment," *Weavings,* 1995, *10*(6), p. 10.

4 Job, *Guide to Spiritual Discernment,* p. 82.

5 Wright, "Passing Angels," p. 10.

6 Frederick Buechner, *Wishful Thinking: A Theological ABC* (San Francisco: HarperSanFrancisco, 1973), pp. 118–119.

Part Two

1 Benedicta Ward (trans.), *The Sayings of the Desert Fathers* (Kalamazoo, Mich.: Cistercian Study Series 59, 1975), p. 4.

Chapter Three

1 Benson, *Between the Dreaming and the Coming True*, p. 110.

2 Buechner, *Wishful Thinking*, p. 85.

3 Robert Benson, *Living Prayer* (New York: Tarcher, 1998), p. 8.

4 Ward, *Sayings of the Desert Fathers,* p. 81.

5 *The Rule of the Society of Saint John the Evangelist* (Cambridge, Mass.: Cowley, 1997), pp. 54–55.

6 Mark Salzman, *Lying Awake* (New York: Knopf, 2001), pp. 76–77.

7 Buechner, *Wishful Thinking,* p. 86.

8 Brother Roger, *The Rule of Taizé* (New York: Seabury Press, 1968), p. 33.

9 Ward, *Sayings of the Desert Fathers,* p. 4.

10 De Mello, *Song of the Bird,* p. 12.

Chapter Four

1 Wright, "Passing Angels," pp. 11–12.

2 Parker J. Palmer, *Let Your Life Speak: Listening for the Voice of Vocation* (San Francisco: Jossey-Bass, 2000), p. 67.

3 Flora Slosson Wuellner, *Prayer, Fear, and Our Powers: Finding Our Healing, Release, and Growth in Christ* (Nashville, Tenn.: Upper Room Books, 1989), p. 67.

4 Wuellner, *Prayer, Fear, and Our Powers,* p. 67.

5 Charles V. Bryant, *Rediscovering Our Spiritual Gifts* (Nashville, Tenn.: Upper Room Books, 1991), p. 44.

6 Flora Slosson Wuellner, *Prayer and Our Bodies* (Nashville, Tenn.: Upper Room Books, 1987), p. 22.

7 Palmer, *Let Your Life Speak,* p. 68.

Chapter Five

1 *Rule of the Society of Saint John the Evangelist,* p. 82.

2 Douglas Wood, *Old Turtle* (Duluth, Minn.: Pfeifer-Hamilton, 1992).

3 Felicity Kelcourse, "Discernment: The Soul's Eye View," in J. Bill Ratliff, ed., *Out of Silence: Quaker Perspectives on Pastoral Care and Counseling* (Wallingford, Pa.: Pendle Hill, 2001), p. 35.

4 Urban T. Holmes III, *Spirituality for Ministry* (New York: HarperCollins, 1982), p. 75.

5 Leo Tolstoy, *Walk in the Light and Twenty-Three Tales,* trans. Louise Maude and Aylmer Maude (Farmington, Pa.: Plough, 1998), p. 260.

6 Richard J. Foster, *Celebration of Disciple: The Path to Spiritual Growth* (San Francisco: HarperSanFrancisco, 1978), p. 69.

7 De Mello, *Song of the Bird,* p. 50.

8 Foster, *Celebration of Disciple,* p. 71.

9 Hermits of Bethlehem, *A Way of Desert Spirituality: The Plan of the Life of the Hermits of Bethlehem* (Staten Island, N.Y.: Alba House, 1998).

10 Kevin W. Irwin, "Lectio Divina," in Michael Downey, ed., *The New Dictionary of Catholic Spirituality* (Collegeville, Minn.: Liturgical Press, 1993), p. 596.

11 Joseph D. Driskill, *Protestant Spiritual Exercises: Theology, History, and Practice* (Harrisburg, Pa.: Morehouse, 1999), p. 93.

12 Julie Vivas, illus., *The Nativity* (San Diego, Calif.: Harcourt Brace, 1986).

Chapter Six

1 David Manuel, *A Matter of Diamonds* (Brewster, Mass.: Paraclette Press, 2000), p. 38.

2 Luibheid, *John Cassian,* p. 70.

3 John O'Donohue, *Aman Cara: A Book of Celtic Wisdom* (New York: HarperCollins, 1997), p. 12.

4 De Mello, *Song of the Bird,* p. 1.

Part Three

1 Ignatius of Loyola, *Spiritual Exercises and Selected Works,* ed. George E. Ganss (Mahwah, N.J.: Paulist Press, 1991), p. 162, no. 175.

Chapter Seven

1 Jonathan Edwards, *Religious Affections* (Minneapolis, Minn.: Bethany House, 1984), p. 26.

2 Luibheid, *John Cassian,* pp. 65–66.

3 Ignatius of Loyola, p. 163, no. 179.

4 Palmer, *Let Your Life Speak,* pp. 44–46.

5 Ignatius of Loyola, p. 164, no. 181.

6 Ignatius of Loyola, p. 202, no. 317.

7 Ignatius of Loyola, p. 165, no. 185.

Chapter Eight

1 Patricia Loring, *Spiritual Discernment: The Context and Goals of Clearness Committees* (Wallingford, Pa.: Pendle Hill Publications, 1992), pp. 15–16.

2 Howard H. Brinton, *Friends for 300 Years* (Wallingford, Pa.: Pendle Hill Publications, 1964), p. 28.

3 Jan Hoffman, *Clearness Committees and Their Use in Personal Discernment* (Philadelphia: Twelfth Month Press, 1996).

4 Hoffman, *Clearness Committees,* p. 24.

5 Loring, *Spiritual Discernment,* p. 24.

6 Parker J. Palmer, *The Courage to Teach: Exploring the Inner Landscape of a Teacher's Life* (San Francisco: Jossey-Bass, 1988), p. 153.

7 Loring, *Spiritual Discernment,* p. 25.

8 Loring, *Spiritual Discernment,* p. 18.

9 Flora Slosson Wuellner, "Were Not Our Hearts Burning Within Us?" *Weavings,* 1995, *10*(6), pp. 27–36.

Chapter Nine

1 Howard Thurman, *Meditations of the Heart* (Richmond, Ind.: Friends United Press, 1953), pp. 178–179.

2 David Baily Harned, *Patience: How We Wait upon the World* (Cambridge: Cowley, 1997), p. 7.

3 Søren Kierkegaard, *Purity of Heart Is to Will One Thing* (New York: HarperTorchbooks, 1938), pp. 101–102.

4 Kierkegaard, *Purity of Heart,* pp. 217–218.

5 Job, *Guide to Spiritual Discernment,* p. 26.

6 Harned, *Patience.*

7 Rainer Maria Rilke, *Letters to a Young Poet,* trans. M. D. Herter Norton (New York: Norton, 1934), p. 35.

8 Archibald MacLeish, *J. B.* (Boston: Houghton Mifflin, 1956), p. 153.

9 Harned, *Patience,* p. 62.

10 William A. Barry, "Discernment of Spirits as an Act of Faith," *Presence,* 2001, 7(3), p. 16.

11 Kenneth Grahame, *The Wind in the Willows* (New York: Bantam Books, 1982), p. 108.

12 Grahame, *Wind in the Willows,* p. 108.

13 Grahame, *Wind in the Willows,* p. 109.

14 Grahame, *Wind in the Willows,* pp. 109–110.

15 Grahame, *Wind in the Willows,* p. 112.

16 Grahame, *Wind in the Willows,* p. 113.

17 Grahame, *Wind in the Willows,* p. 113.

18 Barry, "Discernment of Spirits," p. 16.

Chapter Ten

1 Barry, "Discernment of Spirits," p. 13.

2 Thomas Merton, *Pax Christi* (Erie, Pa.: Benet Press, n.d.).

3 Charlotte Lyman Fardelmann, *Nudged by the Spirit: Stories of People Responding to the Still, Small Voice of God* (Wallingford, Pa.: Pendle Hill, 2001), p. xxii.

4 Fardelmann, *Nudged by the Spirit,* p. 262.

5 Suzanne G. Farnham, Joseph P. Gill, R. Taylor McLean, and Susan M. Ward, *Listening Hearts: Discerning Call in Community* (Harrisburg, Pa.: Morehouse, 1991), p. 45.

6 Ward, *Sayings of the Desert Fathers,* p. 139.

7 Farnham, Gill, McLean, and Ward, *Listening Hearts,* pp. 47–48.

8 Gerald G. May, *The Awakened Heart* (San Francisco: HarperSanFrancisco, 1991), p. 130.

9 Farnham, Gill, McLean, and Ward, *Listening Hearts,* p. 49.

FOR FURTHER STUDY

Discernment

Barry, W. A. *Paying Attention to God: Discernment in Prayer.* Notre Dame, Ind.: Ave Maria Press, 1990.

Job, R. (ed.). *A Guide to Spiritual Discernment.* Nashville, Tenn.: Upper Room Books, 1996.

Johnson, B. C. *Discerning God's Will.* Louisville, Ky.: Westminster John Knox Press, 1990.

Luibheid, C. (trans.). *John Cassian: Conferences.* Mahwah, N.J.: Paulist Press, 1985.

Silence and Prayer

Maas, R., and O'Donnell, G.O.P. (eds.). *Spiritual Traditions for the Contemporary Church.* Nashville, Tenn.: Abingdon Press, 1990. (Practicum 2: "The Pure Gold of Silence")

McPherson, C. W. *Keeping Silence: Christian Practices for Entering Stillness.* Harrisburg, Pa.: Morehouse, 2002.

Taylor, B. E. *Silence: Making the Journey to Inner Quiet.* Philadelphia: Innisfree Press, 1997.

Vest, N. *No Moment Too Small: Rhythms of Silence, Prayer, and Holy Reading.* Cambridge, Mass.: Cowley, 1994. (Chapter 1: "Silence")

Prayer of Examen

Driskill, J. D. *Protestant Spiritual Exercises: Theology, History, and Practice.* Harrisburg, Pa.: Morehouse, 1999. (Chapter 4: "Spiritual Practices")

Foster, R. J. *Prayer: Finding the Heart's True Home.* San Francisco: HarperSanFrancisco, 1992. (Chapter 3: "The Prayer of *Examen*")

Maas, R., and O'Donnell, G.O.P. (eds.). *Spiritual Traditions for the Contemporary Church.* Nashville, Tenn.: Abingdon Press, 1990. (Practicum 6: "Accountability Before God: The Examen")

Thompson, M. J. *Soul Feast: An Invitation to the Christian Spiritual Life.* Louisville, Ky.: Westminster John Knox Press, 1995. (Chapter 6: "Of Conscience and Consciousness: Self-Examination, Confession, and Awareness")

Gifts

Bryant, C. V. *Rediscovering Our Spiritual Gifts: Building Up the Body of Christ Through the Gifts of the Spirit.* Nashville, Tenn: Upper Room Books, 1991.

Edwards, L. *Discerning Your Spiritual Gifts.* Cambridge, Mass.: Cowley, 1988.

Palmer, P. J. *Let Your Life Speak: Listening for the Voice of Vocation.* San Francisco: Jossey-Bass, 2000.

Wuellner, F. S. *Prayer, Fear, and Our Powers: Finding Our Healing, Release, and Growth in Christ.* Nashville, Tenn.: Upper Room Books, 1989.

Understanding Our Bodies

Farrington, D. K. *Living Faith Day by Day: How the Sacred Rules of Monastic Tradition Can Help You Live Spiritually in the Modern World.* New York: Perigee Books, 2000. (Chapter 8: "Care of Our Body")

Wuellner, F. S. *Prayer and Our Bodies.* Nashville, Tenn.: Upper Room Books, 1987.

Listening to Your Life Story

Palmer, P. J. *Let Your Life Speak: Listening for the Voice of Vocation.* San Francisco: Jossey-Bass, 2000.

Study

Foster, R. J. *Celebration of Discipline: The Path to Spiritual Growth.* San Francisco: HarperSanFrancisco, 1978. (Chapter 5: "Study")

Lectio Divina (Sacred Reading)

Driskill, J. D. *Protestant Spiritual Exercises: Theology, History, and Practice.* Harrisburg, Pa.: Morehouse, 1999. (Chapter 4: "Spiritual Practices")

Langer, R. *Harvest of Righteousness: A Spiritual Discipline of Devotion in the Reformed Tradition.* Louisville, Ky.: Geneva Press, 1999.

Vest, N. *No Moment Too Small: Rhythms of Silence, Prayer, and Holy Reading.* Cambridge, Mass.: Cowley, 1994. (Chapter 2: "Holy Reading")

Wiederkehr, M. *The Song of the Seed: A Monastic Way of Tending the Soul.* San Francisco: HarperSanFrancisco, 1995.

Spiritual Companionship

Foster, R. J. *Celebration of Discipline: The Path to Spiritual Growth.* San Francisco: HarperSanFrancisco, 1978. (Chapter 12: "Guidance")

Guenther, M. *Holy Listening: The Art of Spiritual Direction.* Cambridge, Mass.: Cowley, 1992.

Jones, T. K. *Mentor and Friend: Building Friendships That Point to God.* Batavia, Ill.: Lion, 1991.

Jones, T. K. *Finding a Spiritual Friend: How Friends and Mentors Can Make Your Faith Grow.* Nashville, Tenn.: Upper Room Books, 1998.

Leech, K. *Soul Friend: An Invitation to Spiritual Direction.* (rev. ed.) Harrisburg, Pa.: Morehouse, 2001.

Thompson, M. J. *Soul Feast: An Invitation to the Christian Spiritual Life.* Louisville, Ky.: Westminster John Knox Press, 1995. (Chapter 7: "Companions on the Journey")

Ignatian Spirituality

Dyckman, K., Garvin, M., and Liebert, E. *The Spiritual Exercises Reclaimed: Uncovering Liberating Possibilities for Women.* Mahwah, N.J.: Paulist Press, 2001.

Ganss, G. E. (ed.). *Ignatius of Loyola: The Spiritual Exercises and Selected Works.* Mahwah, N.J.: Paulist Press, 1991.

Green, T. *Weeds Among the Wheat: Discernment: Where Prayer and Action Meet.* Notre Dame, Ind.: Ave Maria Press, 1984.

Silf, M. *Inner Compass: An Invitation to Ignatian Spirituality.* Chicago: Jesuit Way, 1999.

Clearness Committees

Farnham, S. G., Gill, J. R., McLean, T., and Ward, S. M. *Listening Hearts: Discerning Call in Community.* (rev. ed.) Harrisburg, Pa.: Morehouse, 1991.

Hoffman, J. *Clearness Committees and Their Use in Personal Discernment.* Philadelphia: Twelfth Month Press, 1996.

Loring, P. *Spiritual Discernment: The Context and Goals of Clearness Committees.* Wallingford, Pa.: Pendle Hill Publications, 1992.

Palmer, P. J. *The Courage to Teach: Exploring the Inner Landscape of a Teacher's Life.* San Francisco: Jossey-Bass, 1998.

Patience

Harned, D. B. *Patience: How We Wait upon the World.* Cambridge, Mass.: Cowley, 1997.

Palmer, P. J. *The Active Life: A Spirituality of Work, Creativity, and Caring.* New York: HarperCollins, 1990.

THE AUTHOR

Debra K. Farrington is a wise writer, popular retreat leader, and publishing insider with a growing following. She is the publisher of Morehouse Publishing. She was manager of the Graduate Theological Union Bookstore in Berkeley, California, and has published in *Spirituality and Health, Catholic Digest, The Lutheran, U.S. Catholic, Alive Now, Publishers Weekly,* and many other magazines and journals. This is her fifth book.

INDEX

72–81; of God's will, 3–25; hearing heart and, 3–25; Ignatius' methods of, 142–157; imagination exercises in, 153–157; as lifelong process, 46–47; at major crossroads, 134–137; through paying attention, 71–91; practicing, importance of, 20–21, 34, 50–51; through prayer, 53–69; prayer service for, 213–220; process of, 11–12; responsibility for co-creating the world and, 21–23; seeing and, 13–16; soul friends for, 118–126; spiritual directors for, 126–132; through study, 93–112; tests of, 194–211; tools for, 49–132; uncertainty in, 23–24, 191–193

Drained, feeling: failure to use one's gifts and, 77; nonalignment with God's will and, 8–10

Dream, of failing to use one's gifts, 74–75

Dreamer, God as, 13

Driskill, J., 105, 109

Dry periods, in silent prayer. 61

Du Bois, W.E.B., 185

Edwards, J., 137, 140, 157

"Ebenezer Scrooge," 155

Egotism: danger signs of, 117; as obstacle to discernment, 18–19; spiritual community and discernment of, 115–118

Elders: as guides on the path, 116–117; Quaker, 169; as soul friends, 118

Electronic communications, 176

Elizabeth, the annunciation and, 106–108

Embodiment of God, 23

Emotional breakdowns, induced, 170

Energy: through alignment with God's will, 8–10; confirmation of discernment and, 152–153, 206–207; through using one's gifts, 76, 77, 78–79; pros-and-cons list assessment and, 150

Engagement, 173–189. *See also* Action

Ephesians, 16; 1:17–18, 8

Episcopal Book of Common Prayer, 37, 43, 146–147, 196, 216, 217

Epistles, reading the, 103–104

"Evangelist and Christian," story of, 19–20

Everyday life: decisions in, examples of, 20–21; discerning companions in, 113–132; discernment in, 20–24; enslavement to, 12, 42–45; paying attention in, 71–91; prayer in, 53–69; study in, 93–112; tools for discernment in, 49–132

Evil, heart's desires and, 197

Examen, 56, 66–69; method of practicing, 67–68

Examination of Conscience *(Examen),* 56, 66–69

Excitement, sense of, 206–207

Exodus, 103

Expectant waiting, 161. *See also* Patience; Silence

Expectations: failure to use gifts because of, 76–77; letting go of, 36–37

Eyes and ears of the heart, 13–16

Face, hiding and revealing, 54

Family: confirmation by, 208–209; impact of personal change on, 39–40

Fardelmann, C., 194

Farnham, S., 199, 204, 207

Fear: of change, 201; of silence, 57

Feelings: balancing reason and, 139–149; being fooled by, 139–140, 152; confirmation with, 151–153, 206–207, 210–211; of consolation *versus* desolation, 151–153, 200; dangers of ignoring, 141–142; paying attention to, in *Examen* prayer, 66–67; paying attention to, in silent prayer, 60; role of, in discernment, 11; study and, 95–96; of unhappiness, 200

Fees, for spiritual directors, 130–131

Feminine Christ-image, 112

Habits, difficulty of breaking, 35–40

Hamster-on-a-wheel routine, 115

Harned, D., 177, 181–182

Hatred, responsibility for, 22

Healing: body wisdom and, 81–82; openness practice for, 62–65; praying for, after *Examen* practice, 68

Hearing heart. *See* Heart

Heart, 3–25; ancient Hebrews' view of, 4; the attentive, 71–91; cognition and, 95–96, 105; discerning companions and, 113–132; discernment through, 4–25; the engaged, 173–189; God's will and, 8–13; hardened, 15–16; the hearing, 3–25; learning with the, 93–112; new eyes and ears of, 13–16; opening, through devotional reading, 105–112; the prayerful, 53–69; Solomon's request for, 3–4. *See also* Desires, heart's; Discernment

Hebrews, ancient, 4, 95

Herbert, G., 163, 201

Hermits, 115–118

"Hero," story of, 17–19, 116, 132, 140–141, 152, 197, 208

Hiding from God, 54

Hindsight, 86

Hippo, Augustine of, 33, 200

Hoffman, J., 162

Holmes, U., 95–96

Holy Bible, 44

Holy Listening (Guenther), 126

Homeless, working with, 73, 84

Hope, God's desire and, 8, 12

Icons, 111–112

Identity, foundational, 30–31

Idols, ignoring the world's, 41–47

Ignatius, Saint, 135, 142–157, 200; life of, 142; *Spiritual Exercises* of, 142–157. *See also* *Spiritual Exercises*

Illness, 81–82, 84

Images: focus on, in silent prayer, 60; visualization of, in intercessory prayer, 63–65

Imagination exercises, in Ignatius' second method of discernment, 153–157

"In" crowd, 169

Inadequacy, sense of, 207

Indifference, practicing, 153

Individualism, 17, 44, 132

Inner Teacher, 162

Intellect. *See* Reason and logic

Intercessory prayer, 62–63; openness practice with, 63–65

Interpretation, in scripture study, 98–103, 106–108

Intuition: balancing reason and, 137–157; preference for, 139–140, 142; role of, in discernment, 11. *See also* Feelings

Ireland, 118

Irwin, K., 105

Isaiah: 2:3, 155; 55:3, 72

Isaiah, Second Song of, 216, 217

Isolation, 22

Japanese Americans, World War II internment of, 169

J.B. (MacLeish), 181

Jefferson, T., 204

Jefferson Bible, 204

Jeremiah 42:3, 125

Jerusalem Bible, 72

Jesus: prayer practice of, 58; on seeing, 14–16; silence and solitude of, 58; in the wilderness, 42, 43

Job, 179–180, 181; 7:7–8, 179–180; 9:24, 180
Job, R., 32, 178
Job seeking, 76. *See also* Vocation or career
John, 107; 6:15, 58; 8:31–32, 102; 15:4, 206;
    16:4–8,12–13, 217
1 John 4:1, 141
John of the Cross, 113
Johnson, S., 107
Jonah, 196
Joseph, Abba, 62
Journal writing: with body wisdom practice, 84, 85;
    with *Examen* prayer, 67
Joy: gifts and, 76, 77, 78–79; as sign of confirma-
    tion, 152, 206–207, 210–211
Judgment, refraining from: by clearness committee,
    164; by soul friends, 122–123
Judgment day, imagining, 156
Judgmental/punishing/wrathful image of God, 4–5;
    as barrier to discernment, 28–31, 100–101;
    conflict between compassionate/loving image of
    God and, 99–101; Examination of Conscience
    and, 66
Justice, people as co-creators of, 21–23

Kelcourse, F., 94
Kempis, T. à, 3
Ken, T., 82
Kierkegaard, S., 177
Kindness, ripple effect of, 22
King James Bible, 144
1 Kings 3, 3–4
Knowing, letting go of, 61–62, 63

Lamott, A., 27, 28, 46
Laws, following: as barrier to discernment, 28–29,
    45, 100–101; using discernment *versus,* 16;
    God-image and, 28–29, 99–101

Leading, fulfillment and, 194
Learning, with the heart, 93–112. *See also* Study
Lectio divina, 105. *See also* Devotional reading
Lenses: clarifying, through study, 97–103; God-
    images and, 98–103; seeing with, 96–103;
    sources of, 96
Lesbians and gays, 102
Let Your Life Speak (Palmer), 71, 77, 87
Letter of Barnabas 21, 148
Letters to a Young Poet (Rilke), 180–181
Letting go: intercessory prayer and, 62–63;
    openness and, 61–65; surrender and,
    31–34
Life story review, 86–91; questions for, 88–89
Light: call to action and, 187–189; visualizing God
    as, 63, 64
Lisieux, Thérèse of, 122
List, pros-and-cons, 139, 147–153
Listening: in clearness committee, 164, 166–167;
    of soul friends, 121, 128
Listening Hearts (Farnham), 199, 204, 207
Literature, sacred reading of, 110–111
Little Prince, The (de Saint-Exupéry), 13–14
Living Prayer (Benson), 55, 202–203
Logic. *See* Reason and logic
Long-term results, 209–211
Longfellow, H. W., 178
Lord's Prayer, The, 44, 63, 97, 219
Loring, P., 159, 163, 165, 166–167, 169
Love, feelings of, as sign of confirmation, 152,
    210–211
Love, God's. *See* Compassion and love
Luke, 15, 103; 1, 106–109; 1:35–38, 106; 4:42, 58;
    6:46, 27
Luther, M., 105, 109
Lying Awake (Salzman), 59

MacLeish, A., 181
Mark, 103, 107; 1:35, 58; 6:45–46, 58; 8:17–18, 15–16; 10:21, 183
Mary, the annunciation and, 106–108
Matthew, 103; 1:18, 107; 13, 14; 13:3–8, 143; 13:3–15; 14, 36–38; 14:23, 58; 14:28–31, 36; 18:20, 114, 161; 19:16, 45; 20, 20; 20:30–34, 15; 22:37, 4
May, G., 205
Meditation, sacred reading as, 105–106, 110
Memories of God (Bondi), 29–30, 94–95
Merton, T., 192–193
Midwives, spiritual directors and, 126
Mind, clearing the: in *Examen* prayer, 67; in silent prayer, 59–60
Mirroring, 167
"Mole" and "Rat," 183–188
Monasteries: service to others and, 198–199; spiritual community and, 116
Monastic rules and guides, 31–32; sacred study and, 104, 105; silence and, 57
More, T., 180
Moses, 99, 174, 176, 196, 201, 207, 210
Moses, Abba, 18, 200–201
Motives, testing of, 199–202
Moving, true *versus* false motives for, 200–201
Murder mysteries, 110–111, 113–114
Mystery, prayer and, 53–54

Nativity, The (Vivas), 108
New Dictionary of Catholic Spirituality, 105
New Testament: discernment based on, 204–205; on God's desire, 7; on seeing, 14–16; suggested readings in, 103–104
New Year's resolutions, 35
Newton, J., 54

Noise, habituation to, 56–57
Nudged by the Spirit (Fardelmann), 194
Numbers, 103

Objectivity, in Ignatius' method, 145–146
Observers, soul friends as, 123
Obstacles. *See* Barriers to discernment
"Odd Couple, The," 174
O'Donohue, J., 119
Old Testament: discernment based on, 204–205; suggested readings in, 103
Old Turtle, 93–94, 95
Openness: in Ignatius' first method, 145–146; in Ignatius' second method, 154; in intercessory prayer, 63–65; methods of practicing, 63–65; prayer practice of, 61–65
Orthodox Christians, 111
Overwhelm, dealing with, 150–151
Oxford English Dictionary, 180

Pachomius, 116
Paintings, for sacred study, 107–108
Palmer, P., 71, 77, 87, 145–146, 159–161, 166, 167
Pambo, Abba, 57
Parables, 14
Parental influence, on God-images, 29–30, 34–35, 94–95
Partners with God. *See* Co-creators with God
Patience: action and, 173–175, 181–189; as catalyst for action, 181–189; challenges of, in modern world, 176–177; challenges of living with uncertainty and, 178; Christian theology and discourse on, 178–181; defined, 180; Job and, 179–180; loving the questions and, 180–181; negative view of, 179; preference for action *versus,* 174–175

Patrick, 46

Patterns, difficulty of changing, 35–40

Paul, 12, 16, 23, 74

Pausing, 177

Paying attention. *See* Attention, paying

Peacefulness, sense of: as confirmation, 152, 153, 206–207, 210–211; as feeling of consolation, 152, 153; pros-and-cons list assessment and, 150

Peak moments, practice and, 34

Peekaboo game, 54

People of color, 102

Peter, 36–38

Pherme, Theodore of, 50–51

Physical body. *See* Body

Pilgrims' Progress, The (Bunyan), 19–20

Place, for prayer, 59, 64, 67

"Portly," 183–188

Possibilities: imagination of, 153–157; remaining open to, 145–146

Poverty, patience and, 179

Power, as Western cultural value, 41–45

Practice: in *Examen* prayer, 66–67, 68; importance of, 20, 34, 50–51; in prayer, 55–56; in silent prayer, 60; tools for, 49–132

Prayer, 53–69; concepts of, 53–56; for confirmation, 151–153; everyday practices of, 53–69; *Examen* (Examination of Conscience), 56, 66–69; for God's guidance, in Ignatius' method, 146–147; intercessory, 62–65; limited ideas of, 53–54; openness, 61–65; regular practice of, 55–56; sacred reading and, 105; silent, 56–61

Prayer, Fear, and Our Powers (Wuellner), 74–75

Prayer and Our Bodies (Wuellner), 81

Prayer Service for Discernment: liturgy of, 214–220; use of, 65, 213

Preferences, personal: for action *versus* patience, 174–175; for reason *versus* intuition, 139–142

Presence of God: developing awareness of, in *Examen* prayer, 66–67; pervasiveness of, 6–7; reflecting on past experiences of, 88–89; waiting for, in silent prayer, 60–61

Pride, gifts and, 73–74

Pridefulness, busyness as, 177

Pros-and-cons list, 139, 147–153; assessment of, with reason, 149–151; sample questions for, 147–148; weighting in, 149

Protestant Spiritual Exercises (Driskill), 109

Proverbs 3:6, 144

Psalms, 204; 19:14, 58; 28:7, 21; 31:3, 8; 33:20–21, 176; 34:1, 214; 37:4, 8, 21; 37:7, 180; 37:23, 132; 40:1, 176; 43:3–5, 32; 46:10, 57; 48:17, 101; 51:6, 11; 56:15, 214; 62:1, 57; 69:13, 66; 84, 214–215; 85:8, 161; 119:105, 98; 139:23, 146; 143:8, 29

Punishing God. *See* Judgmental/punishing/wrathful image of God

Quakers. *See* Society of Friends

Question clarification: for clearness committee, 164–165; in Ignatius' method, 144–145

Questioning: by clearness committee, 165–166, 170–171; by soul friends, 119, 121–123

Questions, loving the, 180–181

"Rat" and "Mole," 183–188

Reading. *See* Devotional reading; Scripture; Study

Reason and logic: assessing pros and cons with, 149–151; balancing intuition and, 137–157; dangers of ignoring, 139–140; in Ignatius' *Spiritual Exercises,* 144–153; preference for,

139–140, 141–142; pros-and-cons list and, 147–153; role of, in discernment, 11
"Reasonable," problem of defining, 149
Recollection, 165
Reconciliation, Taizé community of, 198–199
Recorder role, 164
Red Cross, 188
Reflection, in clearness committee, 167
Relationships: abusive, 35; changing, 150–151; draining, 10; gifts and, 75; with spiritual directors, 132
Relaxation: in openness practice, 64; in silent prayer, 59
Religious art, 111–112
Researching and planning, 150–151
Resistance: dangers of, 9–10; of family or friends, 39–40, 208–209; to temptation, 41–47
Responsibility, for co-creating God's world, 21–23
Results, long-term, 209–211
Retreat centers, finding spiritual directors through, 131
Retreats, emotional breakdowns in, 170
Review: *Examen* prayer for, 65–69; of life story, 86–91
Richard of Chichester, Saint, 210
Ridley, N., 164
Riévaulx, Aelred of, 127
Right answer. *See* Accuracy of discernment; Confirmation; Uncertainty
Rightness, sense of, 197
Rilke, R. M., 180–181
Ripple effect, 22
Roger, Brother, 198–199
Roman Catholics, spiritual directors and, 130
Romans: 1:11–12, 119; 12:2, 151

Rootlessness, 200–201
Rossetti, C., 121, 131
Rule of St. Benedict, 31–32
Rule of Taizé, The, 61
Rule of the Society of Saint John the Evangelist, 93
Rules, following. *See* Laws, following
Running away, 199–200

Sacred reading, 105–112. *See also* Devotional reading
Sacred word, focus on, 60
St. Benedict, Rule of, 31–32
Salzman, M., 59
Sarah, 181
Satan: listening to ego and, 19; world's temptations and, 42
School, recurring dream about, 74–75
Schooling, early, 99–100, 102
Schoolteachers, 40
Scott, C. H., 17
Scripture: Bible sections to start with, 103–104; clarifying God-images with, 98–104; contextual reading of, 205; courses in, 104; critical reading of, 98–103, 106–108; devotional reading of, 97–98, 105–112; four-stranded garland method of reading, 109–111; getting started with, 103–104; interpretation of, 98–103, 106–108, 204–206; study of, 93–112, 204–206; study of, with others, 104, 205; as test of discernment, 202–206; uncertainty in, 102–103; violence in, 204–205. *See also* Study
Secrecy, 117
Seeing: *Examen* prayer for, 65–69; through new eyes and heart, 13–16
Self-employment, choosing, 38–40, 195
Self-exposure, prayer as, 54

Self-image: childhood development of, 30; difficulties of changing, 35–40

Self-sufficiency, 44

Seminaries, finding spiritual directors through, 131

Serving others, as test of discernment, 197–199

Shadow side, of gifts, 80

Silence, 55; in clearness committee meeting, 165, 166–167; discomfort with, 56–57; empty periods of, 61; listening to, 56–61; methods for practicing, 59–60; in prayer services, 65; Quakers' use of, 161, 165, 166–167

Sitting position, for prayer, 59, 67

Skills: gifts *versus,* 76–77, 79, 80; listing, 79; transferable, 76

Society of Friends: balance of individual and community in, 161–162; clearness committee history in, 163; clearness committee technique of, 159–171; elders in, 169; leading in, 194; stories of discernment in, 194. *See also* Clearness committee

Society of Saint John the Evangelist, The Rule of the, 93

Solitude, 58

Solomon, 3–4

Soul friends, 118–124, 132; characteristics of, 120–124; choosing, 120–126; frequency of consultation with, 125–126; getting started with, 124–125; number of, 120; role of, 118–120; spiritual directors *versus,* 128

Spirit, fruits of the, 209–211

Spiritual autobiography, 88

Spiritual directors, 126–132; characteristics of, 128–131; choosing, 130–132; defined, 126; fees of, 130–131; levels of guidance given by,

128–129; resources for finding, 131; value of, in discernment, 126–128

Spiritual Directors International, 131

Spiritual Exercises, The (Ignatius), 135, 142–157; balance of reason and feelings in, 157; confirmation step in, 151–153; first method of discernment in, 142–153; imagination exercises in, 153–157; openness and objectivity in, 145–146; overview of, 142–143; praying for God's guidance in, 146–147; preparation for, 143; pros-and-cons assessment in, 147–153; question clarification in, 144–145; reason-focused method in, 144–153; second method of discernment in, 153–157

Spirituality for Ministry (Holmes), 95–96

Stained-glass windows, 111

Star Trek: The Next Generation, 202

Stress, 81, 83, 84, 85, 129

Study, 93–112; of art works, 107–108, 111–112; critical, 98–103, 106–108; devotional reading and, 97–98, 105–112; getting started with, 103–104; God-images and, 93–95, 98–104; heart and, 95–96, 102; interpretation and, 98–103, 106–108; lenses and, 96–103; sources of, 96, 103–104, 110–111. *See also* Devotional reading; Scripture

Suchocki, M. H., 7

Surrender: difficulties with, 31–34; gifts of, 31–34; gradual process of, 32–34

Taizé, The Rule of, 61

Taizé community, 198–199

Tanner, H. O., 107, 112

Temperature, 59, 64, 84

Temptations of the world, resisting, 41–47

Ten Commandments, 99
Ten Commandments, The, 72
Teresa of Avila, 89, 178, 182
Tests of discernment. *See* Accuracy of discernment;
  Confirmation; Uncertainty
Theodore of Pherme, 50–51
Theopilus, Abba, 57
Thérèse of Lisieux, 122
"Three Little Pigs," 182–183
Thurman, H., 173
Time, test of, 209–211
Time frame: for big decisions, 137; for body
  wisdom practice, 84, 85; for consulting soul
  friends, 125–126; for consulting spiritual direc-
  tors, 132; for *Examen* prayer, 67, 68; for fruits
  of the Spirit, 209–211; for life story exercise,
  90; for prayer practices, 68–69; for silent
  prayer, 59, 60. *See also* Patience
1 Timothy 4:14, 75
Tolstoy, L., 96–97
Tools of discernment: everyday, 49–132; for major
  transitions, 133–189; overview of, 50–51;
  paying attention as, 71–91; prayer as, 53–69;
  spiritual companions as, 113–132; study as,
  93–112
Transferable skills, 76
Transitions, major. *See* Decisions, big
Traveling Mercies (Lamott), 27, 28, 46
Truth, measure of, 161–162

Uncertainty: about accuracy of discernment, 23–24,
  191–193; about scriptural interpretation,
  102–103; action and, 185; patience and, 178;
  test of time and, 209–211
Understanding, of soul friends, 119–120

Unhappiness, 199–200
Uniqueness, of gifts, 73–74
Unitarian congregation, 99
University of Wittenberg, 105
Unknown, leaving the comforts of normal and,
  35–40
Unworthiness, feeling of, 12, 30, 101

Values, cultural. *See* Cultural values, Western
Verification. *See* Accuracy of discernment; Confirmation
Violence: in the Bible, 204–205; evil and call to,
  197; responsibility for, 22
Vision, gift of, 101
Vivas, J., 108
Vocation or career, 20; body clues about, 82–83,
  84; difficulties of changing, 38–40; discernment
  of, 45–46; fulfillment of heart's desires and,
  195–196; gifts and choice of, 75; openness to
  possibilities of, 145–146; question clarification
  for, 144; service and, 199; spiritual directors'
  guidance in, 127–128
Volunteer work, 199

Water, God as, 7
Wealth, as Western cultural value, 41–45
Wesley, C., 198
Western values. *See* Cultural values, Western
Wilderness, Jesus in, 42, 43
Williams, W., 208
Wind in the Willows (Grahame), 183–188
Women, surrender and, 33
Work, enslavement to, 42–44. *See also* Vocation or
  career

World Council of Churches, 1983 General Assembly, 194

Wrathful God. *See* Judgmental/punishing/wrathful image of God

Wright, W., 42, 71

Writing career, 38

Wuellner, F., 74–75, 81

Www.sdi.org, 131

Other Books of Interest

Learning to Hear with the Heart:
Meditations for Discerning God's Will
Debra K. Farrington
$15.95 Hardcover
ISBN: 0–7879–6716–5

An inspirational, personal guide
to discerning God's will for your life

In this companion guide to *Hearing With the Heart,* Debra K. Farrington, helps faithful Christians to hear, see, feel, and think with the heart, for it is through this process that we are able to attune ourselves to the Spirit and to what God wishes for each of us. This companion for the discernment journey guides readers to come to understand God's will, not only for the big decisions about jobs, relationships, and purpose, but also for smaller everyday matters. Drawing on stories, scripture, prayer, and questions for reflection, Debra K. Farrington encourages readers to be fuller and more joyful participants in discerning the shape and direction of their lives and in learning to live closer to God.

Suitable as both a companion book to *Hearing with the Heart* and as a stand-alone, this inspirational guide to the discernment process can be used for individual devotional reading as well as small group work. However it is used, *Learning to Hear with the Heart* will help readers find their way to the truth of their lives by learning to listen for the still, small voice.

DEBRA K. FARRINGTON (Harrisburg, PA) is a writer, popular retreat leader, and the publisher of Morehouse Publishing. Her work has appeared in a wide variety of publications including *Spirituality and Health, Catholic Digest, U.S. Catholic, The Lutheran, Publishers Weekly,* and many others.

[PRICE SUBJECT TO CHANGE]